STOP Buying Health Plans and START Buying Health Insurance!

STOP Buying Health Plans and START Buying Health Insurance!

◆

An Easy-To-Understand Guide to the How and Why of Consumer Directed Healthcare

(HSAs, HRAs and Deductible-First Medical Insurance)

Written By:
Jeffrey Ingalls and Daniel Ritter

iUniverse, Inc.
New York Lincoln Shanghai

STOP Buying Health Plans and START Buying Health Insurance!

An Easy-To-Understand Guide to the How and Why of Consumer Directed Healthcare (HSAs, HRAs and Deductible-First Medical Insurance)

Copyright © 2007 by Jeffrey B. Ingalls

All rights reserved. No part of this book may be used or reproduced by any means, graphic, electronic, or mechanical, including photocopying, recording, taping or by any information storage retrieval system without the written permission of the publisher except in the case of brief quotations embodied in critical articles and reviews.

iUniverse books may be ordered through booksellers or by contacting:

iUniverse
2021 Pine Lake Road, Suite 100
Lincoln, NE 68512
www.iuniverse.com
1-800-Authors (1-800-288-4677)

The views expressed in this work are solely those of the author and do not necessarily reflect the views of the publisher, and the publisher hereby disclaims any responsibility for them.

ISBN: 978-0-595-42985-1 (pbk)
ISBN: 978-0-595-87326-5 (ebk)

Printed in the United States of America

This book is for those who heard the whispers of 'they're making the biggest mistake of their lives' as they quit their job and walked out the door to start their own business.

This book is for those who will one day change the world because they would rather dream than sleep.

This book is for those who have failed a million times but have never stopped asking the question, 'but what if I could?'

Lastly, this book is for the small and mid-size employer. Our passion is to continuously strive to find and implement the best solution for this specific marketplace. We feel this book and the consumer directed healthcare movement is the next step in that mission.

Contents

Introduction xiii

The Short Version *1*

Part One The Setup *5*
    1.1 So Who Are We Here To See? 7
    1.2 What We Have Here Is A Big Bowl of Alphabet Soup 8
    1.3 Good. Fast. Cheap. 9
    1.4 Does This Sound Familiar? 10
    1.5 We're Right Back Where We Started From. 12
    1.6 We're Going To Need To Wage A War … but a gentle one 13

Part Two The Problems *15*
    2.1 Maybe Three's A Crowd 17
    2.2 We Took A Wrong Turn And We Just Kept Going 18
    2.3 The Annual "Going Out Of Business" Sale. 21
    2.4 The HMO Forgot It's Wallet (again) So You're Really Paying 22
    2.5 Now You See It, Now You Don't 24
    2.6 What Are We Fighting For … Really? 26
    2.7 Medical Care Has Become "Like A Box of Chocolates …" 27
    2.8 Don't Take Our Word For It—Take Yours 29
    2.9 And The Diagnosis Is … Entitlement Mentality (Designer Envy). . . . 30
    2.10 Health Crisis or Healthcare Crisis? 31
    2.11 We Know A Guy Who Knows How To Solve A Problem. 32

Part Three The Solutions 33

    3.1 Let's Get Started 35
    3.2 If You Want Something Done Right, Do It Yourself. 36
    3.3 Presenting Healthcare Insurance ... Redesigned. 38
    3.4 Not Less Care, Just Different Care. 40
    3.5 "Let Me See, Let Me See" 41
    3.6 This Better Be Good 42
    3.7 We'd Like To See A Menu, Please. 43
    3.8 He-Said, She-Said Evidence Beats Defense 45
    3.9 Maybe The Hare Does Beat The Tortoise In A Race. 46

Part Four The Products 47

    4.1 Cost Sharing Plans. 49
    4.2 Deductible-First Health Insurance 50
    4.3 The Two Kinds of Deductibles 51
    4.4 It's All About The MOOP. 52
    4.5 Health Reimbursement Arrangements (HRAs) 52
    4.6 Flexible Spending Accounts (FSAs) 53
    4.7 Medical Expense Budgeting. 54
    4.8 Health Savings Accounts (HSAs) 55
    4.9 Remember the Now and Later? 56
    4.10 Wellness Programs and Health Incentive Accounts (HIAs) 57
    4.11 Ok, Ok—Here's The List 58

Part Five The Roadmap 61

    5.1 This Is Not The Equivalent Of The Pet Rock 63
    5.2 Welcome to Wherever You Are 64
    5.3 The Natural Evolution. 66
    5.4 The Road To Somewhere 68
    5.5 We Don't Need No Uneducated Consumer (No Employee Left
        Behind) 71
    5.6 Show Me The Money 73
    5.7 Fund, Fund, Fund 'Till Daddy Takes The T-Bird Away 76

5.8 How To Set The Table..77
5.9 What You Won't See 85
5.10 If It Ain't Broke, Steal It...86
5.11 If We Were In Charge..87

About the Authors......................................89

Acknowledgements

A special thank you to those who knowingly or unknowingly supported and/or assisted us in this process: Doug Belden, Dino Stampone and the entire staff at The Stratford Financial Group, Carl DeRiso, Scott Peloquin and Bradley Tamulski.

Also, we extend our thanks to the countless websites, magazines, organizations, authors and professionals who consistently bring this subject to the forefront.

Introduction

Ever notice how almost every Beach Boys song is about surfing? (Surfin' Safari, Surfin' in the USA). Every song is about summertime fun and has a positive outlook on life. So how come every time the next big wave in healthcare (or health insurance) comes along, nobody wants to hear about anything even remotely related to a surfboard. We all tend to duck and hide until the last possible second, when that tsunami size wave is about to crush us before we even consider embracing the idea of "riding it."

Well, we're here to tell you that the next big wave is here and this book can teach you how to surf. Consumer Directed Health Care, with its Deductible-First Health Insurance, Health Savings Accounts and Health Reimbursement Accounts, is the wave of the future or at least until the government takes it over (but that's a different book altogether!).

So grab a board and let's head where the waves are and learn how to stop buying <u>health plans</u> and once again, start buying <u>health insurance</u>.

Many books, articles and consultants will approach this topic primarily with information about Health Savings Accounts (HSAs). This book intends to explore the problems with our current system, the solutions required to correct those problems, the products to enable a solution to be implemented and a roadmap to get from wherever you are to consumer directed healthcare.

The Short Version

This is managed care.

Managed Care Plan
(example – PPO or POS based)

In-Network	Out-of-Network	Prescription Card
100% Coverage	70% Coverage	$10/$25/$50
	Deductible	

This is consumer directed healthcare.

Deductible-First Health Insurance
(example – PPO or POS based)

Health Savings Account	In-Network	Out-of-Network	Prescription Card
	100% Coverage	70% Coverage	$10/$25/$50
Pre-Tax Money		High Deductible ($1,100 to $5,000)	

Remember this if you remember nothing else—the deductible. The deductible first is the crux of consumer directed healthcare. It just takes your managed care plan and puts it up on a higher shelf. That's it. The rest of this book will just provide further explanation and understanding of that one, simple point. Health Savings Accounts are a secondary benefit of consumer directed healthcare, not the solution. It's the deductible that will fix our system of employer-delivered group health care.

And it is not something to be feared.

Part One

The Setup

1.1 So Who Are We Here To See?

This book is for the following people:

Employers. As both employers and insurance professionals, we see the burden of most business' second largest business expense as very challenging and often suffocating to the growth and maturity of an entrepreneurial vision. From the stereotypical trend-setting West Coast employers to last-to-try it East Coast employers, we all are skeptical, to varying degrees, to embrace a new healthcare concept. This book intends to help, in a small way, keep the dream alive and kicking for the small and mid-size employer.

It's for the early adopters and those who would rather "wait and see." There are some who will want to start implementing change tomorrow and others who will prefer to see what it all looks like when the dust settles. This book is for both of you.

It's for the real stars of the show—the Human Resources professional. If you are an HR professional exclusively or if the HR function is just one of the many hats you wear in a given day, this book is for you. The success of consumer directed healthcare will rely heavily upon the awareness and education provided to participants before, during and subsequent to a program's implementation. That job will often fall directly on top of the pile, already placed squarely on your shoulders.

It's for those who believe we should have a single payer system or government run healthcare. Many say consumer directed healthcare is our last hope of doing it ourselves, the end of the line for the employer-delivered system of healthcare. Some say government involvement would be the best thing since sliced bread while others say it would be the equivalent of buying healthcare from the Department of Motor Vehicles (DMV). This book does not intend to become political. After all if it did, I'd have nothing to argue with complete strangers about at Starbucks. Right?

1.2 What We Have Here Is A Big Bowl of Alphabet Soup

So before we zip up our wetsuits and take our first surfing lesson, let's get a few definitions out of the way. They may not mean a whole heck-of-a-lot right now but they will shortly, depending on how fast you read. As you know or as you'll soon find out, almost everything in the insurance industry is an acronym (It's an evil plot created by insurance agents and brokers to take over the world with our super-cool lingo.) Anyway, here is what we'll be talking about:

<u>Consumer Directed Healthcare (CDHC)</u>—a movement to promote consumer awareness of the costs and quality of healthcare services and create a free enterprise system where providers compete for your business by lowering prices, improving quality and creating options

<u>Deductible-First Insurance</u> or <u>High Deductible Health Plan (HDHP)</u>—an insurance program with no first dollar benefits (no co-payments); insurance with a minimum of an $1,100 individual/ $2,200 family deductible applied to both in-network and out-of-network services and prescription drug benefits before any reimbursement is paid; this is the required insurance program in order to establish a Health Savings Account; referred to in this book as the new Deductible-First medical insurance

<u>Health Savings Account (HSA)</u>—an account containing pre-tax employee dollars funded by the employee (or in some cases the employer) which can be used to reimburse eligible medical expenses (for example—the deductible in a High Deductible Health Plan) or saved for retirement (similar to an IRA or 401k)

<u>Health Reimbursement Arrangements (HRA)</u>—an arrangement between the employer and the employee whereby employer dollars (and only employer dollars) are established to reimburse employees for pre-determined, specified medical expenses (for example—deductibles, generic drug co-payments)

<u>Cost-Sharing Health Plan</u>—a managed care plan that typically maintains co-payments for office visits and prescription drugs but places a deductible (for example—$500 up to $2,500) and a lower reimbursement percentage (for example—90% down to 50%) as opposed to providing 100% coverage for services typically including outpatient procedures and surgeries and inpatient hospitalizations

<u>First Dollar Benefits</u>—this refers to managed care plans such as a PPO, POS or HMO plan that offers coverage subject to a co-payment or in many instances

offer 100% coverage; the most important aspect of the plan is that there is no upfront deductible before the plan reimburses for medical care

Indemnity Plan—also referred as hospitalization and major medical; the type of health insurance program that pre-dated managed care; the use of a deductible and coinsurance without the use of a network of contracted providers to reimburse eligible medical expenses; the old version of deductible-first medical insurance

In-Network—when speaking of a managed care plan, this refers to the use of the insurance company's contracted network of providers for medical care

Out-of-Network—when speaking of a managed care plan, this refers to the use of medical providers who do not belong to the insurance company's contracted network of providers

Managed Care Plan—typically a PPO, POS or HMO healthcare plan (see below)

PPO (Preferred Provider Organization)—a managed care plan that allows employees to visit a contracted network of providers for enhanced benefits or visit non-contracted providers for a lesser benefit; members are not required to choose a Primary Care Physician (PCP) or obtain a referral from a PCP to visit specialists (in-network)

POS (Point Of Service)—a managed care plan that allows employees to visit a contracted network of providers for enhanced benefits or visit non-contracted providers for a lesser benefit; members are required to choose a Primary Care Physician (PCP) and obtain a referral from a PCP to visit specialists (in-network); in-network coverage acts as an HMO (see below) and the out-of-network coverage acts as an indemnity plan

HMO (Health Maintenance Organization)—a managed care plan that only allows employees to visit a contracted network of providers for benefits; the use of non-contracted providers is not covered; members are required to choose a Primary Care Physician (PCP) and obtain a referral from a PCP to visit specialists (in-network)

Open Access—the removal of the requirement to obtain a referral from a Primary Care Physician to visit a specialist (in-network); this term often applies to POS and HMO plans

1.3 Good. Fast. Cheap.

It's the oldest business adage in the book—not this book but "the" book. Good, fast, cheap. You can have any two of the three but you can't have all three. You can have it good and fast but it's not going to be cheap. You can have good and cheap but it's not going to be fast. You get the picture. So what's the parallel to healthcare or an employer-sponsored medical insurance plan? The three aspects would change to (1) what the employer pays in premium, (2) what the employees' pay via contributions and (3) the plan design. Once again, you can only control two out of the three. Managed care allowed you to control all three for quite some time so if you're used to controlling all three, it's not your fault. It's probably more the insurance industry's than yours.

If you're convinced you still need to control all three, you can and to a much more logical and sustainable degree. Consumer directed healthcare will allow you to do what managed care no longer is capable of—controlling what the employer pays, controlling what the employees pay and controlling the plan design. Consumer directed healthcare takes the best of the past and present healthcare systems and creates a new, brighter future. We'll get in to exactly what that means as we both autopsy the current managed care concept and pull back the curtain on the newest concept in healthcare, consumer directed healthcare.

According to Fortune Small Business magazine, Health Savings Accounts (and consumer directed healthcare) are just what the doctor ordered and the newest way for businesses to manage the soaring costs of healthcare insurance. You can decide for yourself in a little over an hour when you finish reading this book.

1.4 Does This Sound Familiar?

Employers take a listen—hear anything that rings true to your method of handling renewals? Your broker delivers an awful renewal of 15% if you're lucky (typical managed care trend is 12%-18%). He shows you lesser benefits at a lesser cost or similar benefits with another carrier at either a slightly lesser cost than your renewal offer or in a good number of instances, an even higher cost then your renewal. You "shop around" and meet with other brokers to see if your guy or gal missed anything. This was once a very productive exercise, as the group medical insurance market, in its totality, was often not fully explored by one broker or firm. The "shopping around" often brought to light previously unquoted carriers and products and plans. As we all have seen with insurers, the market has shrunk whereas in many states the number of "players" (insurance companies) can be counted on one hand. This all leads to the unfortunate conclusion that most likely, your broker showed you all there was to see, until now, until the birth of consumer directed healthcare.

The above example we firmly believe applies to the vast majority of employers. There is no benefits strategy, no multi-year approach, and no predictable benefits in the years to come. There is a reactive system is place. We receive awful renewals and react and put something in place that will "sort of" work for a year. We run around like Chicken Little because the sky is falling—your second largest business expense is going up and up and up.

At renewal time, employers and brokers alike all do the same thing. We run around looking for the best benefit plan at the lowest price. We do it year after year after year. What we should be doing is implementing a multi-year strategy that will provide predictable benefits consisting of the right mix of healthcare insurance plans at the most level and controlled cost. Consumer Directed Healthcare provides us the best tools, so far, to do just that.

So what's the problem? There are a few and we'll talk about them all but right now the problem is this. Like any industry, salespeople will only sell what they know will work and more importantly, what they understand. You can't sell what you can't explain. You can't sell a plasma TV if you can't turn it on and show a customer how it works. Right now many brokers combat your interest in consumer directed healthcare with, "it doesn't work just yet", "the pricing is not there yet", "the East Coast is not yet ready for a new concept", "your employees will hate it", "it's only for the wealthy (and healthy)." You would do or say anything to divert the attention back into your comfort zone. As with anything else, you can't buy what nobody is selling.

What we'll be talking about will require a new method of thinking, a paradigm shift in the mind of the consumers—the employers and the employees. Employers need to stop co-habituating inside the box with most insurance people and engage this concept, step outside the box for a moment and find the way consumer directed healthcare will work for them.

1.5 We're Right Back Where We Started From

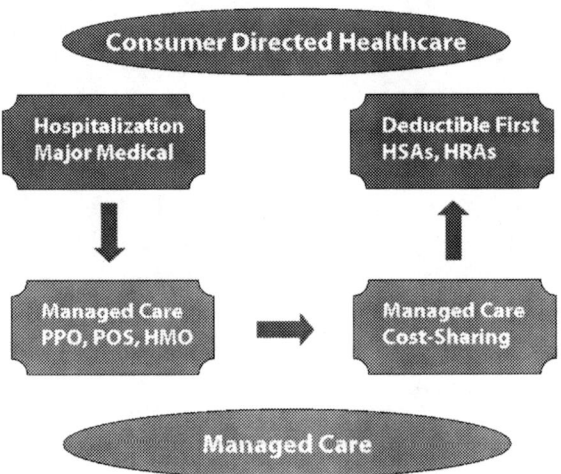

Back in the 1980s, most likely you had what was called an indemnity plan; it was also called hospitalization and major medical insurance. Translated from Insurance to English this meant that for the most part, you paid a reasonable deductible then the plan paid a percentage of your covered charge. There were no first-dollar benefits, no co-payments, no provider networks, and no managed care.

Then came then 90s and managed care. PPO, POS and HMO became the trend, the new, fancy way to control healthcare costs by managing the care to varying degrees. People were incented by low premiums to purchase health plans that used a network of providers (in-network) that you could see for very minimal co-payments. The insurance carriers kicked down the doors of resistance with a deal too good to be true—low premiums and even lower costs to receive care. They eliminated the need for us to worry how much medical services actually cost.

As we entered the millennium, more and more employers had gravitated or would gravitate towards more restrictive managed care plans. In other words, by now HMOs were the standard. We had trained ourselves to diminish our desire to see non-participating doctors and found ourselves exclusively using provider networks and paying co-payments for almost everything.

So here we are or welcome to wherever you are. It's the new millennium and managed care is no longer working. Premiums increase and increase and benefits decrease and decrease. The solution is the best of both worlds—a Deductible—First or High Deductible Health Plan (HDHP) coupled with a Health Savings Account (HSA). This approach looks more like the deductible and coinsurance approach from the 1980s blended with the best aspects of managed care—namely, preventive care and provider network discounts.

This new solution puts the power back to the patient. It, to a degree, diminishes the role of the insurance company as the third party acting on your behalf and let's you take the wheel. It encourages participants to take an active role. Does that intimidate you? It shouldn't. We are all intelligent, educated consumers who are fully capable of letting it be known what we want, what we need and when the price is right. Afterall, we exhibit this ability in almost every other marketplace besides healthcare.

1.6 We're Going To Need To Wage A War ... but a gentle one

This book is going to define the current healthcare system's problems, the proposed solutions to those problems, explain the products you can purchase should you agree with the solution and provide a roadmap to get from wherever you are to consumer directed healthcare. Having spent much of our careers in the insurance industry in an element of group insurance sales and customer service, we know first-hand, as well as anyone, that healthcare is a personal and emotional item or event. We are also fully aware that the customer's (or in the case, the reader's) perception is all that matters. Let us repeat that, it's all that matters. But in order to fully explore this topic, we need to entice a gentle and productive argument between managed care and consumer directed healthcare.

In an attempt to provide you a tool for de-personalizing the subject, we are going to do what more skillful writers have done for centuries—hide behind a chapter ending summary with flashy graphics. We were going to use fictional characters. We were going to use comic book superheroes and villains named The Consumer Crusaders and The Legion of Healthplan Doom. But we decided against it. Regardless and hopefully, this summarization will still allow you to achieve a fresh and objective perspective on the subject and provide an overview of the following two sections of this text.

14   STOP Buying Health Plans and START Buying Health Insurance!

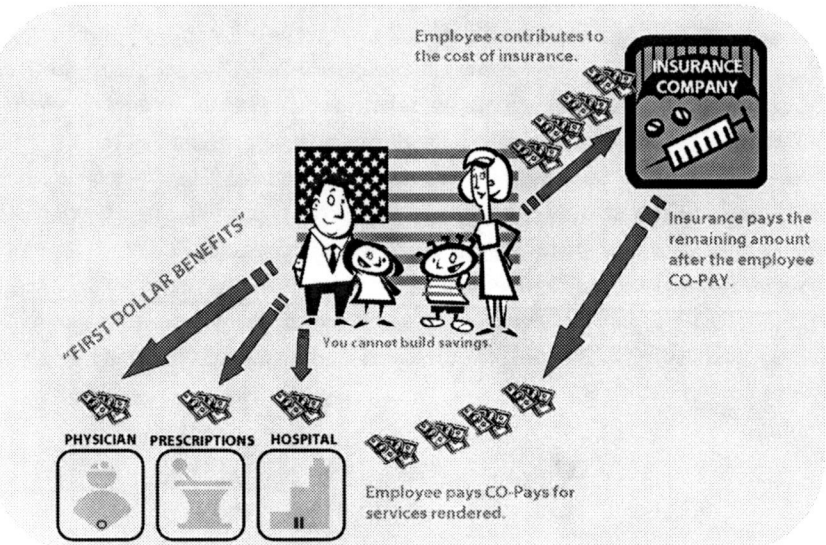

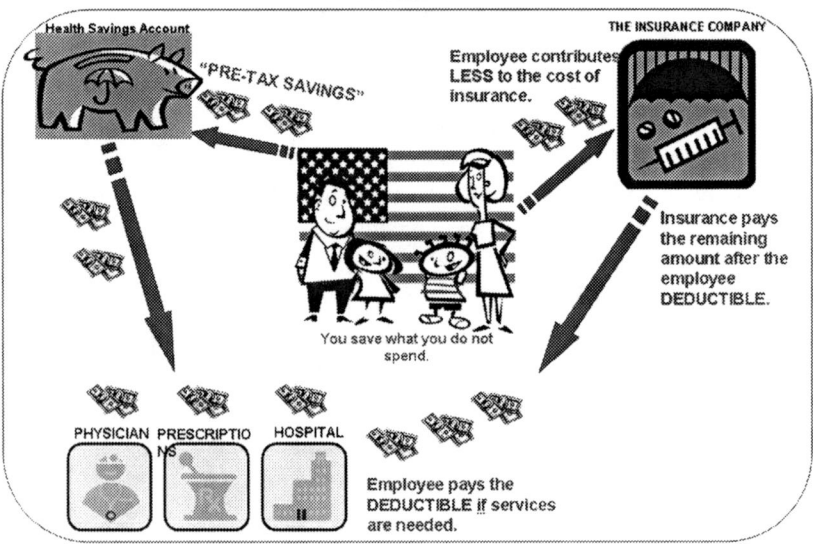

Part Two

The Problems

 We need to STOP thinking that obtaining the plan with the lowest copay at the lowest cost is the measure of a properly constructed health insurance program.

 We need to STOP being told what providers to go to, how much we need to pay and take responsibility for our health and our healthcare.

 We need to STOP treating healthcare as an entitlement but as a system in which we all need to take ownership and an active, engaged role.

2.1 Maybe Three's A Crowd

Scott Atlas, MD in his book Power to the Patient sums it up best when he writes, "The third party system of payment—the absence of direct payment from patient to doctor for most medical expenses—has shielded Americans from considerations of cost and imparted (created) the illusion that someone else is paying for medical care. The forces of supply and demand (free enterprise) have become lost amid the sea of governmental regulation and oversight in the third party system. The essential step to remedy this is to change the nature of healthcare insurance so that patients make direct payments to their heath care providers."

In today's managed care world of PPOs, POS plans and HMOs, the insurance company acts as the third party. We, the consumers, the healthcare users are the first party and our chosen medical providers and facilities are the second party. We've been trained to pass all of our concerns to the third party, our insurance company or HMO. We mail in our premium and in doing so we also leave our concern for responsibility, for appropriate care, for quality of care and any consideration of cost we might have once had neatly folded at their doorstep.

The third party insurer acts as an event planner of sorts as they use your money, your premium to make all the arrangements. They tell us how much we need to pay in the form of a co-payment for office visits, for outpatient procedures, for inpatient hospitalizations and for prescription drugs. They also tell the providers how much they'll be paid for the array of medical services they provide in a given day. The end result is the third party holds all the cards, we have no idea how much we're being charged and our providers have no idea how much they're being paid.

We've done what we have been told, like good boys and girls and in the process; we created a system of healthcare "users". We are all driving blindfolded until our renewal when we reopen our eyes and see the same wall we crash into year in and year out. And who's there to greet you?—the third party. The insurance companies or HMOs have no choice but to point the finger at you, comfortably place the blame in the passenger seat next to you and glance knowingly at the price increase that's been waiting all year for you to arrive. Let's investigate this car crash of a healthcare system a bit deeper, piece-by-piece, foot-by-foot and see how this game of Pin The Tail On The Donkey started.

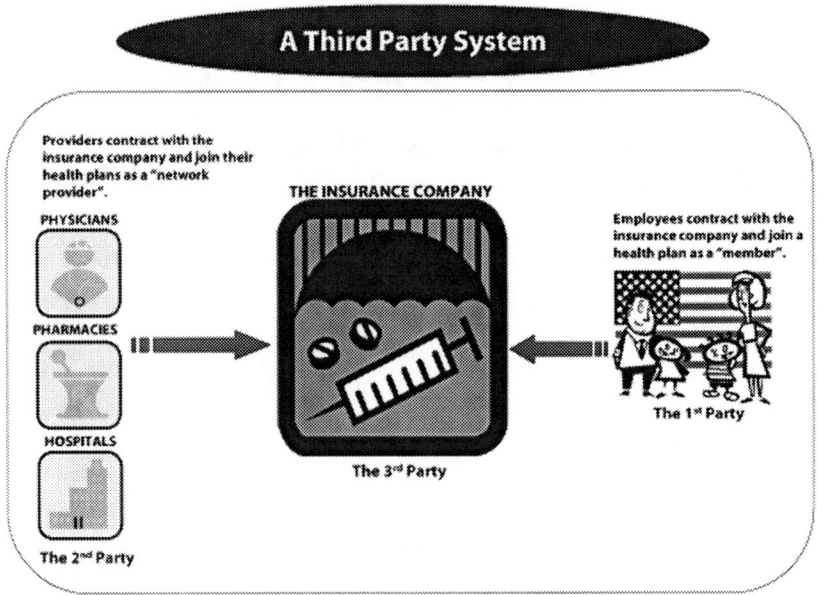

2.2 We Took A Wrong Turn And We Just Kept Going

Insurance is meant to cover the "what if", the "might just happen to me". That's what it's always been really good at—protecting against the big stuff that might just happen to our health, our car or our house. They collected a small, palatable amount of premium from a large number of insureds and paid the few that had major claims during the course of the year. That's their original function, their road best traveled. Somewhere they exited the highway like Dennis Miller commentating on Monday Night Football or Pamela Anderson trying to act, they strayed from their primary focus, the thing that they're really good at. Where? Why? When did medical insurance cease to be a financial vehicle designed for protection and become a very personal, emotional consumption. We'll tell you and do our best to translate the itinerary from Insurance to English.

Back in the 1980s before the advent of managed care, we all maintained what we called indemnity plans or hospitalization and major medical. There were no co-payments, provider networks or first dollar benefits—no 100% coverage right off the bat. We paid reasonable premiums and for the most part had reasonable renewals and predictable, future benefits. The justification for contradictory increases was the misfortune of incurring large claims or evident health conditions in your group.

We paid a reasonable deductible and once we satisfied the deductible, the insurance paid the lion's share percentage of our future claims (we paid the remaining percentage) up to a maximum out of pocket. A typical example would have been a plan with a $200 annual deductible then 80%/20% (insurance company/you) reimbursement or co-insurance and a $1,200 annual maximum out of pocket. This seems almost ancient at this point but this perceivably simplistic approach to healthcare had many positives and here they are (here comes the bullet points!)

- We knew how much medical services cost because we had to pay for them often at the time the service was performed.
- We were involved in our care because for the majority of the year until our maximum out of pocket was met, we shared in the cost.
- We dealt directly with our doctors and providers and they dealt with us. For the most part there was a direct transaction between the provider of the service and the consumer or patient.
- The patient (the insured) budgeted and paid for the routine stuff, the lower cost more likely medical services and the third party (the insurance company) paid for the major stuff, the most expensive and catastrophic medical services. They stayed in the back seat, choosing to not ride shotgun until the big claims occurred, when the out of pocket maximum was reached.
- It was called major medical not minor medical and we focused on the plan's maximum out of pocket (or MOOP).

Then along came managed care and supersized health insurance as we knew it.

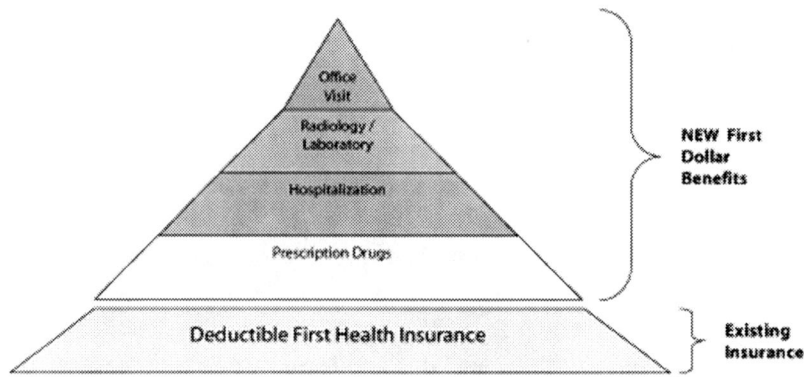

BAM! It created a health insurance <u>plan</u>. Come join us, we have a plan that's cheaper, that's better and you'll be healthier and wealthier. It took what was already there and added several layers of first dollar benefits. Insurance companies went out and created provider networks. They said hey look, Mr. Physician you need patients and we have the ear of the insured patients. We'll drive them to your practice but in return we want a discount off your normal price. One physician said ok, then another, then another until most of them were forced to join networks in order to compete.

Managed care offered enhanced coverage for the services that were formerly subject to an annual deductible, coinsurance and the annual out of pocket maximum. The newly formed managed care health plan covered them at 100% subject to a co-pay and redirected our focus as consumers. When it first came out, you could now see a physician for $5 and purchase any prescription on earth for about $2. We now had insurance for the small stuff, the likely medical services. Managed care eliminated much of the up-front thought process, the consideration of cost. The trade-off is we were now joined at the hip to the plan. They would manage our care, they would decide what was appropriate care not for their insureds but for their members. People resisted the change, concerned that they would be "John Q'"d or disallowed care they one day might desperately need by the evil, money motivated HMO. To combat the resistance, the managed care companies kicked down the doors with the aforementioned lower costs of care (100% coverage, minimal co-pays) and even lower premiums. The government even joined the battle by mandating that groups of certain size offer an HMO as part of their employer-sponsored medical coverage.

But managed care definitely had its pros, its elements of concern that cannot be ignored or downplayed even with 20/20 hindsight.

- They developed networks of providers that were willing to discount their fees. Most importantly on the large claims, inpatient hospitalizations for example.
- Eliminating the cost consideration by offering first dollar benefits on routine medical services and by offering preventive care benefits, they got people to go to the doctor. Co-payments all but dared them to get there. As a result, we were able to treat illnesses sooner and stall or triage their progression.

So here we are, the 21st century and the new healthcare movement is consumer directed healthcare. This movement combines the best aspects of both former systems of healthcare delivery. We'll delve in into this deeper in Chapter 4—The Products but here are the elements of consumer directed healthcare as well as their origins.

Benefits Originating From Hospitalization and Major Medical	Benefits Originating From Managed Care Plans
The up-front deductible is back creating the need for insureds to once again budget and pay for the small stuff.	Patients will have the benefit of pre-negotiated pricing with the network of providers.
Insureds or patients will once again have a consideration of cost and will deal directly with their chosen provider(s).	Preventive care will continue to be covered at 100% as a first dollar benefit.

2.3 The Annual "Going Out Of Business" Sale

According to Organisation for Economic Co-operation and Development Health Data prepared in 1998, healthcare consumers spent considerably less in out of pocket medical expenses in 1998 than in 1988. Inflation, utilization, etc. have all risen in that same timeframe—everything, except our out of pocket. That's obviously out of whack and deserves an explanation for which there is a very legitimate and obvious one when you think about it.

Managed care plans put healthcare on a never-ending sale. Think about it for a moment and I'll use round numbers to simplify but not skew my point. Let's say the average physician office visit costs $100. Managed care networks, the insurance companies' or HMOs' contracted physicians agree to accept $60 for this same office visit. You have a managed care plan with a $10 co-pay. You pay $10 and the insurance company pays the other $50. Paying only $10 for a $100 service is a 90% off sale, a clearance, last stop before the dumpster type sale. That problem in itself spirals off a whole host of other symptomatic problems leading to the impending doom of managed care.

Ever wonder why they use poker chips in casinos as opposed to cash money, dollar bills? Obviously, it's so you disassociate yourself from the chips' monetary value and allow your spending behavior to run rampant. The healthcare consumer or "user" (as we should be deemed in a managed care environment) is altered by the use of co-payments for medical services. One need not be Alex P. Keaton or even a real economist to piece together that the insurance consumer's behavior and mindset is going to be altered after a prolonged period of time under this façade, these "sale" conditions. We no longer place any value on medical services because it's just about the only product or service for which we've decided it's appropriate to abandon any and all consideration for cost we once had. After all, how can you value something for which you continually pay so little and do not maintain the foggiest recollection of its actual price. It's the moral equivalent of handing a toddler a Mickey Mantle rookie card and curiously wondering why he or she is not treating it more carefully and respectfully. Every time we pay a co-pay, we put another crease, another bent corner on our system and delivery of health care.

We've begun to treat our health plan as a rental car or worse yet, an open bar. We paid our cover charge (our premium) and now we have an entitlement mentality. Line 'em up barkeep because I'm going to be here a while. And put away the cheap stuff because I paid my money and now you're buying ... but are they really?

2.4 The HMO Forgot It's Wallet (again) So You're Really Paying

We just used the simplistic example of a $100 office visit with a $60 contracted discounted fee for using the provider network. You paid a $10 co-payment and the insurance company paid the remaining $50. Now stop right there because that's exactly where we lose it! That $50 is our money. It's the premium we pay—the premium difference between the cost of providing catastrophic health insurance coverage and a managed care health plan. They use our money to pay these charges, then they use all the healthy insured's money to pay these claims and then after all other options have been exhausted, they use their own money. If you have an employee only premium of $400 and you don't use $4,800 in medical care services, you just contributed to that fund. Wouldn't you rather handle your own money and pay it out only if you have to?

Small claims create an administrative burden on insurance companies and on your providers' billing offices. They both employ football fields of people to keep track of fee schedules and bill for these small services. Higher employment costs and higher administrative costs translates into higher premiums. With utilization rising steadily year after year, this problem is far from going away.

Switching gears for a moment, let's review the Price WaterHouse Coopers 2006 report on the drivers in healthcare, they claim (no pun intended) every $1 in premium collected is allocated in the following manner:

86%	is spent on pure, claims reimbursement
5%	is spent on customer service, provider support, and specialty programs
6%	is spent to conform to government regulations
3%	is insurance company profit

According to the report, average premium increases have paralleled increases in medical care utilization and pure claims activity and reimbursement. In other words, as utilization of medical services increase or as medical services rendered simply cost more, your premium increases accordingly. This is based on a national average health plan renewal increase of 8.8% in 2004-2005 (that's a little low for us tri-staters, don't you think?). So what is driving the increase? The report states the blame for the increase is divided up as follows:

27%	is the result of general inflation
30%	is the result of healthcare costs increasing in excess of general inflation
43%	is the result of increased utilization

So to summarize, the number one driver of healthcare increases is increased utilization of medical care (which by itself has increased at a rate of more than double inflation). So what medical services are contributing to the aforementioned 86% claims costs:

24%	Physician services
22%	Outpatient procedures and surgeries
18%	Inpatient hospitalizations
16%	Prescription drugs
6%	Durable medical equipment, home health care, etc.

If this report does not dispute the myth that "someone else is paying for medical care" we're really not sure what will. So let's move on.

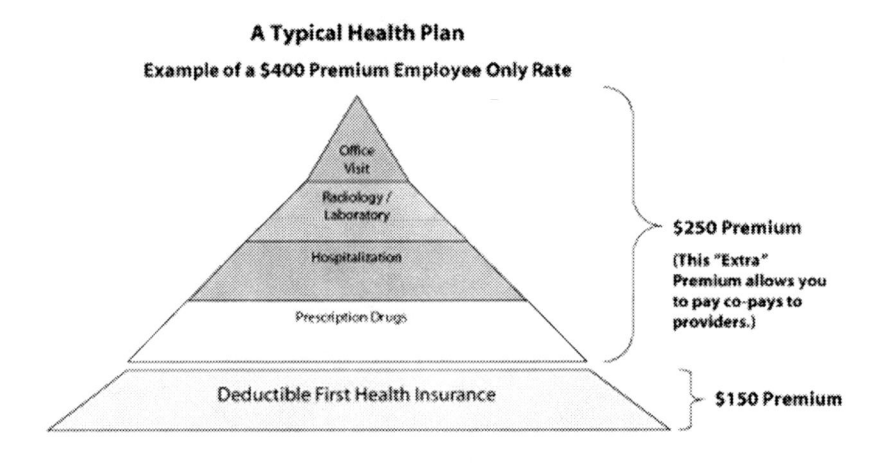

A Typical Health Plan
Example of a $400 Premium Employee Only Rate

- Office Visit
- Radiology / Laboratory
- Hospitalization
- Prescription Drugs

$250 Premium (This "Extra" Premium allows you to pay co-pays to providers.)

- Deductible First Health Insurance

$150 Premium

2.5 Now You See It, Now You Don't

There's another aspect of managed care that has also led us down the Road To Implode. It has to do with an old saying coined by movie mogul, William Goldman—"Nobody Knows Nuthin". He meant it regarding which movie will become the next blockbuster hit. We mean it in regarding the price of medical care services. Consumers do not know how much things cost because managed care has trained them not to care. Physicians, medical providers and facilities would have to consult their fee schedule for your chosen insurer to find out how much they are being paid. Even that assumes they have an updated, current schedule, if they even have a copy at all. The system of managed care and its functionality is dysfunctional at best and would not be tolerated in the marketplace of any other product or service.

Let's put that last statement and the lack of pricing transparency to the test. Let's say Macy's stopped being a clothing store where you select the items you want or need and paid for them in full (either with cash or credit card) immediately at the point of purchase. Let's say they decided to change the clothing industry as we know it, break new ground and offer (you ready for this?) Managed Wardrobe Plans. The people who used to be called customers pay a monthly fee to become a "member". Let's say $350 a month and each time plan members enter the store they pay a shopping fee of $30. And last but not least, they are welcomed to go to Macy's anytime they justifiably feel they are in need of a new article or articles of clothing. Something happens to a suit, they get a new one, etc and etc.

A beautiful Saturday morning rolls around and a member decides he needs new clothes for work. His are old and are on the verge on looking "worn". He enters Macy's, pays his $30 fee and picks out two new suits, five new ties and hey, while he's at it, three pairs of socks. He may not have needed the socks but the choice seemed appropriate at the time. Keep in mind, Macy's has removed all the tags (price tags, brand-name tags, clothing features tags) from their clothes because price is no longer a concern and the other items represent needless quality information at the point of purchase anyway. Macy's personnel makes note of his visit, his new wardrobe selections and he's on his way. A few weeks later he receives an Explanation of Clothing in the mail, which outlines the selections he made that Saturday and lists their actual price. He realizes that the socks he selected cost $24.99 each. He didn't really need those socks and would have definitely passed on them altogether or made a different selection to say the least. Under this new method of clothing purchasing, how long do you think it will be before our plan member:

- Starts going to Macy's a little more often than he used to.
- Notices that his attitude and perception as to appropriate clothing shopping is changing, starts to resent the monthly fee and feels entitled to new clothing for the money he's paying.
- Loses all former knowledge of what a shirt costs, etc.?
- Ceases to be able to determine the value of his clothing selections because has no cost or quality information when he selects them.

- Notices that Macy's is increasing the "back-office" pricing of its clothing and more importantly, their monthly fee.
- Would find it hard to go change his attitude and perception towards clothing and revert to "the old way of doing it".

The lack of pricing transparency causes an issue of major concern as you'll see in a moment.

2.6 What Are We Fighting For ... Really?

One of our wives recently needed a new cell phone, she dropped hers in a bucket of bleach (don't ask). She went to the wireless store and viewed their selection of available phones. Each was neatly and simply displayed and underneath each phone hung a nicely laminated and clear sign that noted the price of each as well as the benefits, features and functionality of the phone. So let's think about this, before making her choice, she could easily weigh both a cost consideration and a quality consideration and make an educated decision.

She could have also consulted the internet and visited a whole host of sites to find out how other consumers are rating these phones, how experts rate the phones and get even more detailed information about her upcoming selection. She could research quality without having to rely on word-of-mouth or gut instinct. She knew what she was getting.

Managed care has extinguished our desire for up-front confirmation of quality. By eliminating the need for cost consideration, quality consideration was the next domino in the line, teetering and waiting to fall. Managed care has taught and led us to become more concerned as to the network participating status of a provider rather than their medical success rate and other quality measures. Do we know any of the following information when we choose a provider for a surgery?:

- The number of times the surgery has been performed
- The number of times the surgery led to a corrected or improved health status
- The number of times a patient died during the surgery
- The likelihood that your exact diagnosis led to surgery in your area versus other areas of your state
- The percentage of times patients may have successfully taken a different path, other than surgery, and achieved successful results

Also, how does this criteria apply to the other suitable surgeons right in the general vicinity of where you work or live. This is referred to as evidence based medicine. Now last time we checked we were not licensed physicians so we are going to leave that statement to be researched further by you, the reader. Suffice to say, our current version of managed care casts an unintentional shadow of doubt on the quality of healthcare we receive. 10% of our claims are due to defensive medicine to act in concert with the lack of medical liability reform and to safeguard providers against malpractice claims. In other words, we need to be concerned about the balancing act our providers undergo. While 100% of their energy should be devoted to providing cost effective, efficient and quality care with the best possible outcomes, they do need to at times, heed to the lure of defensive medicine simply to avoid malpractice claims.

If we had a tool or even an interest in selecting care based upon proposed or proven quality and effeciency, there might be upfront research which might lead to fewer malpractice claims as the substandard physicians, surgeons and medical facilities would be smoked out and exposed by consumers. As of right now, they are as illusive as Osama Bin Laden in the hills of Afghanistan. Getting back to our story, the cell phones in the store ranged from $79 to about $699, if they took away the nice, laminated descriptive signs that included the price, could you value them from worst to best? We are all fighting tooth and nail to hang onto our managed care plans and our beloved co-payments, but should we? What are we really fighting for? Do we know?

2.7 Medical Care Has Become "Like A Box of Chocolates ..."

"Life is like a box of chocolates, you never know what you're going to get". Remember that line? How could we forget Tom Hanks' portrayal of the lovable Forrest Gump. Without a measure of cost consideration and a measure of quality, how do we compare value or worse yet, redevelop a sense of value for medical services. Americans are by far the globe's best purveyors of consumer perceived value in all services and products except healthcare. It is impossible to gauge value without knowledge of price and quality. Just ask the folks on Antiques Roadshow, they'll sing the same song. Our co-pay based managed care plans certainly get us to the doctor and theoretically improved the quality of our healthcare. But did they really and can we think of a better way? A concern needs to be raised as to whether or not we can intelligently say that we obtain the most appropriate and best suited care for our individual needs under this current system.

We must say pulling a one-arm bandit in Atlantic City is starting to feel a lot like picking a specialist out of a provider directory, paying a co-pay and seeing what happens. This is our health and well-being we are talking about and yet we often choose our brand of coffee more passionately and carefully than our medical providers.

The best physicians and surgeons in any given managed care network are being paid basically the same as the worst. Managed care breeds mediocrity and a cattle call volume. It breeds a consultative-type profit center. Under managed care, providers cannot set their own prices and therefore have to resort to increased volume in order to increase the revenue and the financial success of an office. This creates the situation where physicians spend less time with patients which drives malpractice claims opportunity. It has been proven that the more time a physician spends with a patient the less likely that physician is to encounter a malpractice claim. This all comes full circle.

The other option for a medical practice to boost revenue is to resort to "nickel and diming" the consumer or the patient. This is not stated to create a negative perception of medical providers but to paint an accurate picture of the predicament in which they are boxed. Many physicians now bill for the following services:

- Pharmacy refill requests or authorization requests
- Phone consultations
- Disability or Family Leave Forms
- School or Athletic Medical Forms
- After Hours Phone Calls
- Email Consultations

Email consultations? C'mon! We're not concerned that they are billing for them, we're concerned at the fact that they are providing them. Who is managing this kind of care as many of the HMOs have begun to reimburse them as eligible charges? This is not valued medical care. We're pretty progressive people but even we're not ready to be medically treated over the internet nor are we suggesting that you should be either. But that's where we're headed. According to a 2003 report by Solucient, LLC on the National Trends in Healthcare Consumerism, consumers rely more heavily on the internet (37%) rather than their physician (27%) for their source of medical information. If that doesn't send up a flare concerning the amount of time we get with our medical professionals and the quality of our healthcare, we're not sure what will. So let's keep going.

2.8 Don't Take Our Word For It—Take Yours

Great West Healthcare put out a very telling report on the attitudes and perceptions of healthcare consumers both in 2005 and again in 2006. Many of the issues and concerns raised here are quantified in the results of the survey conducted with healthcare consumers just like you.

- Only 25% of healthcare consumers said they were responsible for controlling rising healthcare costs. 61% said insurance companies are responsible. And we thought we didn't want our care managed?
- Only 11% learn the cost of their medical services prior to having the treatment performed.
- Consumers can estimate the price of a new Honda Accord within 5% accuracy, an oil change within 11% accuracy and a Bose music system within 6% accuracy.
- When asked the cost of a routine doctor visit consumers were off by 52%, an Emergency Room visit off by 70% and on a 4-day hospitalization consumers were off by 61%.
- Only 16% of consumers visit their insurance company's website on a monthly or more regular basis. (If you're one of the 84% there are all kinds of tools and stuff on there.)
- Half of all consumers budget $1,000 or less for medical care per year. A surprising number of those budget nothing.
- 60% of consumers think those with a poor (health) lifestyle should pay a higher premium than those who live a healthy lifestyle.
- 95% would prefer cash or a premium reduction incentive to incent a change in lifestyle to promote health and wellness.

As Dr. Phil says you cannot change what you have not acknowledged to be a problem. We have symptomatic problems of pricing transparency and quality control and a value deficiency to top it all off. If I was Dr. Gregory House, I would probably do a differential diagnosis on the white board. Luckily in this case, the underlying cause is pretty evident.

2.9 And The Diagnosis Is …
Entitlement Mentality (Designer Envy)

As said before, managed care created a sale on healthcare which has caused us to neglect price and even the quality of our healthcare. Hopefully, the text cultivated an undeniable argument that you cannot value something without knowledge of price and quality. So what's left to value, is there anything left that we do actually care about? Well there is and it's the only thing that still has a brand name associated with it. In fact, it's written right on the object and glamorized on television like a romance with the heartthrob in a teenage primetime drama. That something is prescription drugs.

Now that healthcare is on clearance, we all want the designer accessories. When it was our money, Macy's brand healthcare was suitable, appropriate and something to be valued. Now that it's their money (perceivably the insurance company's money) only Saks Fifth Avenue, Neiman Marcus, Barney's brand healthcare will do. "It's the only thing that will work for me" is the mantra we hear as we help customers pre-authorize their prescription drugs the insurance companies try to steer them away from with offers of less expensive co-payments and very limited authorization requirements.

It seems as though everyone who had digestive disorders of one kind or another fought to obtain Prilosec a few years ago. Once Prilosec became available over-the-counter, those same patients now required Nexium. It also seems that everyone who suffered from allergies (like we do!) needed the end-all-be-all, Claritan a few years ago now requires Allegra. "It's the only thing that works for me, I've tried all the others" became the new mantra. The need for the good stuff at clearance prices no longer satisfies our insatiable appetite for value; we now need the designer stuff at clearance prices.

A recent study by the Kaiser Family Foundation detailed that for every dollar pharmaceutical companies spend advertising directly to consumers, they obtain a 430% return on investment. More simply put, for every $1 to the networks and the publishers, they get back $4.30. Guess we're not the only ones who have arrived at this diagnosis.

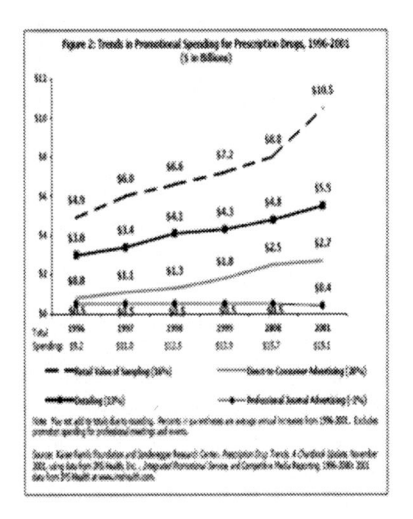

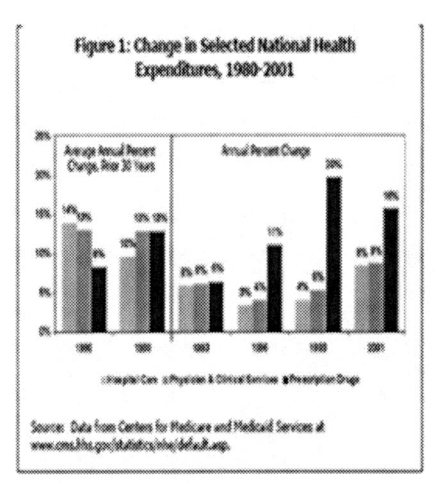

2.10 Health Crisis or Healthcare Crisis?

Just because we have homeowners insurance does not lead us to hold bonfires in our living rooms the night before the big game. Just because we have auto insurance does not mean that we all drive with our eyes closed when we're a bit sleepy. We need to open our eyes and take a more proactive approach to our health. We need to avoid risk, like the insurance companies do, by living a proactive healthy lifestyle even though we have the best reactive healthcare system right out our front doors.

Under our current system, the sick and healthy both pay the same premium and theoretically share the risk spread evenly. Employee contributions are not based upon one's health or one's displayed effort to live a healthy lifestyle. Those costs are generally the same for everyone and most employers have only one medical insurance option in which employees can enroll. There is no financial downside to being sick, no financial upside to living a healthy lifestyle trying to exhibit your control over preventable, chronic illness.

Additionally, we have become accustomed to triage techniques and quarantine options for our illness. Little or no effort is being promoted to prevent illness and avoid later health concerns. We silently sing the praises of "there's a pill for everything" and the "fix me up, doc" as we've become immune to the formerly negative connotation of being on medicine for a prolonged period of time or the balance of our lives. And once we start, it's hard to fathom changing our lifestyle and exhibiting a calculated amount of effort so maybe, just maybe we might not need the medication anymore one day. There's a big difference and an even bigger disparity in the reward associated with avoiding illness through the promotion of wellness versus catching illness early through the use of preventive or managed care.

2.11 We Know A Guy Who Knows How To Solve A Problem

Einstein has two thoughts on solving problems as Robert Hopper points out in his book, The HSA Strategy (his book makes ours look like a pamphlet!). One is insanity is defined as doing the same thing over and over and expecting different results. That is essentially how we handle our managed care renewals. We get increase after increase, purchase another managed care plan and sit and wait with our fingers crossed in vain until next year. WE NEED TO CHANGE OUR PLANS.

Einstein's other school of thought on change is that we cannot solve problems with the same thinking we used when we created them. Managed care and the majority of its elements do not work any longer. First dollar benefits, as we have discussed, do not promote the proper use of health insurance. WE NEED TO CHANGE OUR BEHAVIOR.

In short, we need to stop buying health plans and start buying health insurance and here's what will happen if we do.

Part Three

The Solutions

We need to START demanding information concerning the price and quality of the medical care we receive.

We need to START demanding choices for our medical care thereby driving quality of care up and cost of care down.

We need to START embracing new concepts and develop our own system of healthcare.

3.1 Let's Get Started

There are three main attributes and qualities that need to become evident in the healthcare consumer to not only give consumer directed healthcare its chance to shine but to correct the problems spawned by managed care. First off, we need transparency. We need to be able to see what have not been able to get a good look at in quite some time. We need to move past the iron curtain of the insurance companies' fee schedules so consumers can see what things cost. We also need to demand quality and efficiency information so we can make educated choices about our providers and our medical care.

We need to stimulate free enterprise by dealing directly as the healthcare consumer with the provider of medical services. This will downplay the role of the troublesome third party on the small claims by placing an up-front deductible first(we'll get to that in a second). This will ultimately drive prices down, drive quality up and create choices for the consumer. Continued education and understanding by the healthcare consumers can certainly enact this in the marketplace and awaken the consumer in all of us from the hypnosis created by managed care.

Last but not least, we need to set in motion the necessary shift in attitude and perception to get your arms around this concept and use it to the benefit of both your financial and physical well being. You need to get some semblance of a vision for the future so you can actively participate in the solution and opposed to dragging your heels with the managed care crowd.

We are driving in a James Dean game of chicken with a very stubborn brick on the gas pedal and the cliff clearly in sight. We have to make a choice to hit the brakes and look at this differently because we all know what the other option is and it's not exactly going out in a blaze of glory. It ends with employee layoffs, employers electing to not sponsor a health plan and businesses closing their doors.

3.2 If You Want Something Done Right, Do It Yourself

We need to all become an army of one. We need to re-evaluate this healthcare system and embrace the positives that can come from allowing consumer directed healthcare to shuffle past the moaning and groaning and have its chance to be heard amongst the static. We need to take responsibility and ownership of our health, our healthcare and our health insurance.

Maybe Gordon Gekko (aka Michael Douglas in the 80s flick Wall Street) was on to something when he stood in front of the stockholders and stated triumphantly, "Greed is Good." The depersonalization of medical insurance and the removal of the healthplan mentality from our decision-making process can do a world of good. Instead of attempting to provide the best benefits and richest reimbursement possible for the 10% of our employee makeup that unfortunately contributes to 80% of the total incurred medical claims, let's take a step back. Let's create a plan that tailors to the other 90% of the employees that are either healthy and well or unhealthy but for the most part, well and collectively contribute to only 20% of the total claims.

Create a System For The Majority

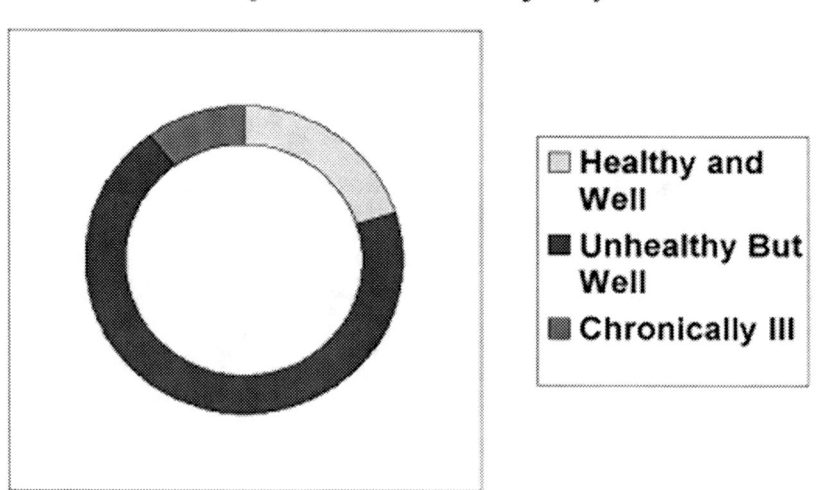

- ☐ **Healthy and Well**
- ■ **Unhealthy But Well**
- ■ **Chronically Ill**

The suggestion here is to let the employees take the wheel, let the consumer drive the bus for a change. One of the many goals of consumer directed healthcare, from a global standpoint, is to afford insureds the opportunity to save money on their ever-rising premiums and provide a level cost of health insurance. By doing so, the premium savings will afford consumers the opportunity to achieve their individual goal. The goal can be to either save that money or reinvest it in their medical care. This statement will be further clarified in the upcoming section as we discuss the use of a deductible first mentality to combat the first-dollar benefits we've grown accustomed to with managed care.

The other global goal of consumer directed healthcare is to allow the consumer the opportunity to manage their own care for the small stuff—office visits, lab tests and the other smaller ticket items. As we stated, managed care took its shot at insuring and managing the small stuff by providing those layers of first dollar benefits on top of the deductible-first, semi-catastrophic plans we once purchased. Consumer directed healthcare saves the consumers the premium dollars associated with providing those first dollar benefits and lets them decide for themselves the best course to chart for their medical care. After all, who do you think the best consumer would be if I provided you the following choices?

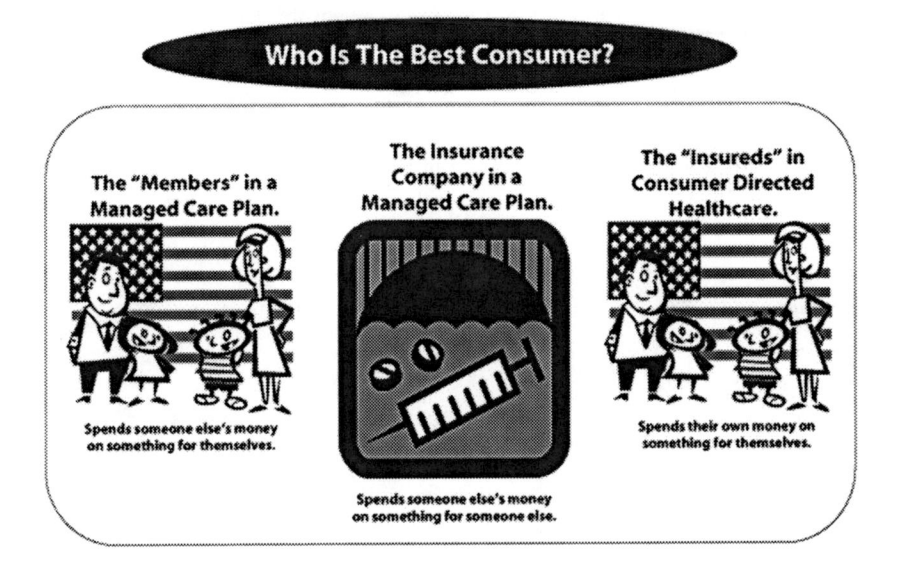

Who Is The Best Consumer?

The "Members" in a Managed Care Plan.
Spends someone else's money on something for themselves.

The Insurance Company in a Managed Care Plan.
Spends someone else's money on something for someone else.

The "Insureds" in Consumer Directed Healthcare.
Spends their own money on something for themselves.

We have to ask ourselves to dissect the many aspects of our current managed care plan as if these were the parts to a new car we were purchasing. It's important to note that managed care can easily draw the comparison to leasing a car as opposed to buying or owning a car. Keep that in mind as we perform this exercise and carry this discussion to future sections of this text dealing with Health Savings Accounts. If the base model of the new car was Deductible-First health insurance and the first dollar benefits of a managed care plan were available for you to purchase a la carte like options on that new car, which options would you purchase and which would you pass on?

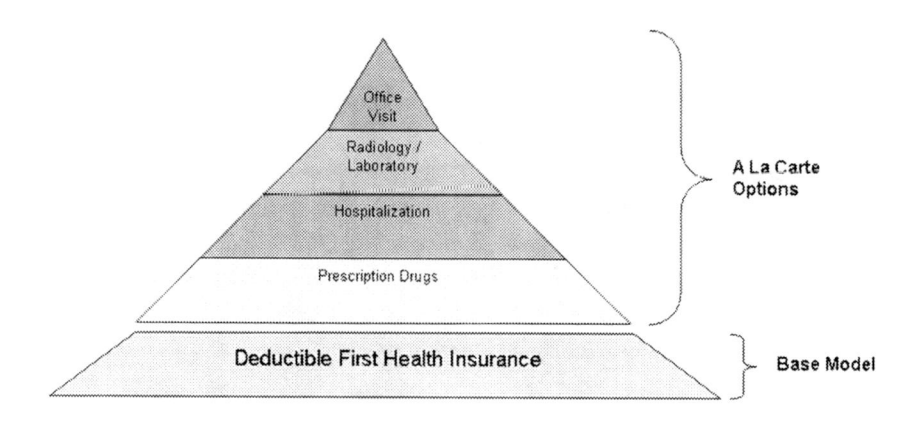

```
                    Office
                    Visit
                 Radiology /
                 Laboratory                      } A La Carte
                                                   Options
               Hospitalization

            Prescription Drugs

      Deductible First Health Insurance          } Base Model
```

Think of it as one would their cable bill. Everything comes in packages—the basic package, the premium package, so on and so forth. Everyone who purchases a package does not really want all the channels that come with that package. Everyone is not going to have a need for all the programming, especially as we go further down the dial. The problem is that's the only way to get the channels we actually so want—to buy a package. The news and the media have all danced around the proposed topic of eliminating the packages and allowing consumers to purchase cable programming a la carte. If you could do that, which channels would you buy and which would you pass on? We are certain the packages and many channels would all but disappear.

The main goal here is to take ownership of our healthcare—the use of our premium dollars, the cost of our care, the quality of our care and the options that are available to us. This movement will push us to exhibit the educated and responsible consumer behavior we already maintain in every other aspect of our lives.

3.3 Presenting Healthcare Insurance ... Redesigned

If consumer directed healthcare was really a brand new line of automobile, as in the aforementioned example, that's probably how it would be introduced in a primetime commercial. The basic consumer directed healthcare plan is a managed care plan just propped up on a foundation. They're the plans we all know with the benefits we're all fighting for just placed on a higher shelf. They look a lot like this.

Deductible-First Health Insurance
(example – PPO or POS based)

Health Savings Account	In-Network	Out-of-Network	Prescription Card
	100% Coverage	70% Coverage	$10/$25/$50
Pre-Tax Money	High Deductible ($1,100 to $5,500)		

This creates Pricing Transparency and Free Enterprise

It's the up-front deductible that strips away the first dollar benefits that managed care built and that places the managed care benefits on a higher shelf. At first glance, our managed care mentality will urge us to look at that deductible in a negative light but if you get one thing from this text, let it be this. That simple deductible can save our health care system. It's the Jaws of Life separating us from the burning wreck of crushed metal that has become managed care. That deductible is the key to unlock the handcuffs of managed care. That deductible, as old-fashioned and uninteresting as insurance itself, will revolutionize the way we use our health care benefits. It will generate free enterprise, demand pricing transparency of medical care services, stimulate quality and will force the medical community to create whatever options and choice we deem necessary.

The deductible first health insurance will bring back the days of old but with a double bonus. The government will allow you to continue to receive first-dollar preventive care benefits as well as allow you to establish an HSA, a Health Savings Account. Employers can fund this account for us or we can fund it ourselves with pre-tax dollars. What does that mean? That means we can take money from our gross income, before taxes are taken out and put it into this account. Remember these deductible first plans are less expensive than managed care plans so employers and employees will have the money to do this. We can use that saved money to pay for medical expenses that are subject to that deductible or just save the money for later medical expenses or retirement. The pre-tax money grows tax deferred and basks in the sunshine of compound interest, just growing and growing and growing.

This will also severely cut back on the administrative burden smaller claims present to our bloated system of managed health care. We can now downsize the administrative staff of our insurers and medical providers and reap the benefit of the resulting savings as medical consumers in the form of lower costs of care, lower premiums and controlled renewals.

It's once again, health insurance and it's redesigned by us, the healthcare consumers.

3.4 Not Less Care, Just Different Care

See, we know what you're thinking, you pessimists. We know because we often frequent your club of nay-sayers ourselves. Many will say that the placement of the deductible on the lower shelves and the managed care benefits on the high shelf (the one you need a step stool to reach) will cause people to stay out of the supermarket all together. Okay, enough with the analogy for a moment. Having to satisfy a deductible will cause people to change the way they think and they way they behave but you have to remember managed care just did not begin yesterday.

We have been trained to go the doctor, to use prescription medicine, to test preventively for illness. Those twenty some odd years of managed care conditioning did not arrive in a moment's notice and cannot possibly leave us in a moment's notice either. We will find a way to continue to receive the medical care we deem appropriate but we will do so in an environment where considerations for appropriateness, quality and price of medical care coincide with the need. We will now question our medical providers' course of care versus our previous method of blindly following his unchallenged discretion. We will now consider the use of generic drugs versus brand-name drugs. We will use our new found voice in this market to demand options for healthcare that we require them at a price that we deem fair. And people will listen.

To prepare for this book, we have combed through anything and everything we could get our hands on relative to consumer directed healthcare. We compiled, amongst countless other media, two six-inch thick binders of written materials concerning this healthcare movement. This was a daily process that consisted of reading reports, articles, professional analysis, government data reporting and insurance company white papers. We did not come across one (and let me repeat that, not one) single report or piece of evidence that proved or even suggested that once an insured is in financial control of their healthcare (insured by deductible-first health care) that patients will neglect needed care, abandon preventive care or consistently choose the lowest cost treatment to save money.

In conclusion, it is obvious that this argument, that was granted admittance even in our minds, is not substantiated by any data, raw or realized. Deductible-first medical care is not going to create an environment where otherwise prudent consumers and patients are going to neglect care. Managed care did its job; it got people to the doctor.

3.5 "Let Me See, Let Me See"

That's what our kids exclaim when they desire to see something they have not been afforded the opportunity to see or even more simply put, to see something new for the first time. That's how we should feel about finally developing a medical care system where pricing is not hidden behind a concrete slab of inefficiency and a human fence of administrative barbed wire.

We should have had this information all along but as we've discussed we had no reason to care. We've theoretically been spending Danny Devito's "other people's money." The domino effect this will have will be staggering on the industry not to mention, fun to watch. We can now demand lower prices and vote with our wallet. This will work and the proof is right here.

Remember when full-body CT scans first came out. They were promoted as the ultimate in wellness, a medical service to be desired by patients and envied by their friends. The initial marketing on this service was for executives—the wealthy and the important. The lure of the scan almost begged the question, are you important enough or of significant enough stature to warrant a full body scan? Scanning centers cultivated the designer envy in all of us and lured the executives in at a price of $1,200 per scan. That was the price and we knew it because full-body preventive scans are not covered by most health insurance plans. So the John Q. Public healthcare consumers grabbed a hold of the megaphone and screamed, we want these too and we want them at a lower price. And what happened? The price is now about $300.

Think of your dental care or your vision care. Many employers provide these ancillary benefits but most dental and vision plans are coinsurance based meaning employees share in the cost of most related services. So again, we're sharing in the cost so we know that without a first-dollar benefit, we have to execute some semblance of a cost consideration and retain knowledge of the pricing or obtain it prior to the services being rendered. Those without employer sponsored coverage pay for these services outright and retain or maintain an even greater knowledge of the associated pricing and an even heightened cost consideration. What's the point? The point is dental and vision related costs of care have remained far more quantifiably controlled as compared to the costs of medical care.

This stuff works. We said it before and we'll say it again, we are all excellent consumers. We just need the tools to allow us to prove it. Medical service pricing hears no voice clearer than that of consumers' indication of supply and demand. If we stop buying health plans and start buying health insurance, our collective consumer voice will have its own primetime special every night of the week.

3.6 This Better Be Good

Armed with pricing transparency, we can use a measure of cost to begin to calculate value. The other factor we need to cultivate is a quality measure so we can insure (no pun intended) that our calculations are accurate and true to our healthcare needs. Consumer directed healthcare provides us the opportunity we desperately need to weigh one provider versus another. More and more web-based tools are being created everyday. Imagine being able to perform the following considerations prior to selecting one medical provider over another:

- Weigh the <u>cost</u> of one provider versus another. For example, the cost of a cesarean section ranges from $1,375 to $1,618 amongst three different Washington, DC hospitals.

- Weigh the <u>patient volume</u> of one provider versus another. If you are having intricate neck surgery, the provider with a full practice is probably the better choice as it would signify trust, positive word of mouth and tactical experience. Conversely, if you have a child with a chronic illness, a skilled pediatrician with less of a patient volume may be the better choice. Those criteria may signify that the provider works alone as opposed to part of a practice and will have more time to spend with patients in need of consistent and frequent care.

- Weigh the prescribed <u>surgical recommendation</u> rate per diagnosis. Does Doctor A recommend surgery twice as frequently as Doctor B? If so, a second surgical opinion may be in order. And geographically speaking, do I live in an area where my diagnosis leads to surgery far more frequently than other areas nearby?

- Weigh the <u>surgical success and complication rates</u> of one surgeon versus another. This is self-explanatory; anyone would want the provider that gets it right the majority of the time.

- Weigh the <u>mortality rates</u> of one hospital versus another. Is the surgical mortality rate of Hospital A is twice that of Hospital B, consumers will begin to select Hospital B consistently enough forcing Hospital B to either drastically improve quality or close its doors. Either way, local quality of care goes up.
- Where do I want to go in an emergency? Beforehand, we should all know the degree to which our local hospitals Intensive Care Unit are <u>staffed</u>? This can not only insure quality, it could save lives.

We no longer need to leave the quality of our health care up to only those who participate in our network of providers, what little word-of-mouth we can drudge up prior to making a decision or worse-of-all, luck of the draw. We can make educated, informed up-front choices based upon the collective data of the healthcare consumer community. More and more information is coming to light each and every day. Just like the sections in this book, price information precedes quality data. Our interest and demand for quality healthcare is long overdue.

Many insurance companies that are proactively and enthusiastically supporting consumer directed healthcare have diminished their customer service staff and replaced them with Treatment Cost Advisors. Now instead of battling legions of customer service representatives over frequent, smaller claims they are become similarly staffed and positioned to help you make up-front, cost effective choices by providing you with a wealth of cost and quality information.

If we stop buying health plans and start buying health insurance, the price of medical care will decrease and the quality of our medical care will increase. The engaged consumer involvement will almost guarantee it. So now that we have pricing information and quality information …

3.7 We'd Like To See A Menu, Please

The third benefit of free enterprise is the creation of choice, the development of options. Once consumers gravitate away from managed care plans and towards consumer directed healthcare, we will all be in deductible first health insurance. That means medical providers will now have to compete for the revenue associated with charges that will be subject to the up-front deductible. Competition, or free enterprise, will create options.

Let's head back to old days when we had deductible and coinsurance, indemnity plans, hospitalization and major medical. The year was 1983 and I (Jeffrey) was just a youngster; I didn't know everything until I was at least 16 (*sic*). My father had a health insurance program with a $100 calendar year deductible and then the plan paid 80%.

Every January, without fail, I would get a cold—runny nose, cough, we all know the drill. Since it was the onset of the year and the deductible was not met, my mother would weigh the options of running me to the doctor versus handling the situation with an appropriate alternative, Sudafed or Robitussin. Typically, Dr. Mom would prescribe the over-the-counter medication and in a few days I would feel better. Most likely Dr. Mom achieved the same result as if I went to the doctor and was issued a prescription, a few days later I would feel better. But there was a thought process there and a weighing of the options. Later in the year and once the deductible had been satisfied, the consideration of cost would diminish to a degree and I would probably have been taken to the doctor. But in my example, the total cost in 1979 was about $3 or $4.

Let's stay with this same example and apply it as a realistic scenario under today's managed care system. My mother would instantly bring me to the doctor (with a $75 network contracted fee and a $30 office co-pay for example) and the physician would in all likelihood prescribe Zithromax (with a conservative retail charge of about $84, a generic equivalent charge of about $42 and a brand-name co-pay for example of $25). This handling of this real-life medical scenario totaled about $159 of which the consumer would have paid $55.

Now let's assume we have a deductible-first consumer directed health care program. It's January 1st and we have not met the deductible. Instead of going to the doctor for what you know is a cold, you head to the MinuteClinic. What's a MinuteClinic you say? CVS, Target, Walgreens and RiteAid have all invested to varying degrees in clinics of this type. This is part of a retail store that contains a supervising physician and nurse practitioners. They treat only 25-40 conditions and have a menu board of prices hanging like the sign in a deli. The average cost of a visit, at the moment, is about $45. They maintain patient records and refer out about 10% of cases as the diagnosis is too severe or outside the realm of their 25-40 chosen illnesses. Many of those same retailers have begun to offer roughly 291 generic drugs for $4 per one-month supply. They are already competing for your dollar and we are not even in deductible-first medical plans yet. Total cost under consumer directed healthcare is $49, $6 dollars less than the managed care example. Not to mention the money you saved in premium.

The effect consumer directed healthcare will have throughout the medical services industry will be astounding. The use of deductible first medical care will create options such as this all throughout the medical service industry. Consumers will be handed price sheets along with the customary insurance forms when visiting a physician's office. Laboratories will begin advertising on television and radio, posting prices on the web and competing for your dollar. Hospitals will carry on in the media about success rates like telephone companies carry on about their lack of dropped calls on your cell phone. Generic drugs will receive the publicity of brand-name drugs and will become the standard when available. Medical providers will compete for your dollar with the two best tools in the box, price and quality. If we will stop buying health plans and start buying health insurance, the consumer will win in the end.

3.8 He-Said, She-Said Evidence Beats Defense

Here is a simple explanation of both defensive medicine and evidence based medicine. Defensive medicine is a practice that physician have been forced to adopt to avoid medical malpractice claims. It may be sending a patient for an extra x-ray or some additional labwork his own expert opinion would otherwise eliminate from your charted course of care. The provider does this so he or she does not have to explain why the unwarranted tests were not ordered should a malpractice claim arise. Evidence based medicine is when a provider marries his own opinion with data collected from a significant number of other patients whom have experienced similar symptoms or conditions and plans a course of action.

Long story longer, the deductible first concept save consumers money when services are rendered, it will also reduce the use of medical services for unneeded, discretionary and defensive treatment. Consumers will now be armed with this information and can voice their opinion as they are educated consumers with a financial stake in how much their medical care will ultimately cost.

Think about it. When we go shopping we want to know what other consumers think. Think of any major retailers' website and there are very often consumer comments at the bottom on any product listing. There you will find real-world, practical reviews of the product, the positives and the negatives from those who have purchased and used the product or service. The same should apply to medical care and will in a consumer directed environment. We want to know what consumers think of Doctor Smith on Maple Street. Does he spend time with his patients? Is he just a walking, talking prescription pad? Does he believe in antibiotics for small children or rather they rough it out in exchange for the thought of a more intensive immune system? We want to know and want to hear it from all of you.

This book keeps walking a fine line between the promotion of evidence-based medicine and the covering of defensive medicine in a veil of negativity. This book does not intend to take the place of medical providers nor does it intend to convey that consumer directed healthcare will replace the thoughts and advice of a provider. It does intend to suggest that we as consumers can collectively voice our opinion based upon experience with a provider's charted course of care and become involved. If we stop buying health plans and start buying health insurance we will become involved as part of the solution as opposed to part of the problem. The net effect? Our involvement will insure quality of care and our involvement will reduce malpractice claims thereby reducing the need for defensive medicine.

3.9 Maybe The Hare Does Beat The Tortoise In A Race

Why? Think staying out of the sun and/or using sunscreen versus a skin cancer screening at the dermatologist. As we've discussed, managed care strove to create a preventive delivery of health care diagnosis and treatment. Many of us still have managed care plans at this point and they all contain a preventive care benefit (PCB)—first dollar, 100% coverage for an annual physical, etc. This is geared more to prevent illness rather than catch illness early; henceforth the name. Even though preventable illness comprises 70% of our total cost of healthcare, why is it then, on average, managed care plans seem to agree that less than 12% of health plan members use their preventive care benefit?

Managed Care may have been designed to be a preventive and proactive delivery of healthcare, but that's not what it looks like today. It is generally a very reactive system; we get sick, then we use our health plan and get our treatment and medications. Consumers need to refocus our culture from an emphasis on disease to an emphasis on living a healthy lifestyle. Our lack of emphasis has led actuaries to predict that the U.S. life expectancy may actually decrease in the near future. Managed care did not accomplish this paradigm shift as we spend just as much today on preventive care as we did fifty years ago.

If we stop buying health plans and start buying health insurance, we will discover the financial downside to becoming ill and reap the rewards of living a healthy lifestyle, both physically and financially.

Part Four

The Products

4.1 Cost Sharing Plans

We've spent a lot of time talking about first dollar benefits and moreover, gravitating away from that particular element of managed care. We wanted to include in this text, an element or a program of consumer directed health care that is often omitted from other sources. It's the cost sharing plan and it's a baby step towards full-blown consumer directed healthcare. Some may argue that is just a way to prolong a move away from managed care but we prefer to think of it as consumer directed healthcare with training wheels.

Let's take a moment and see how a cost sharing plan works. There are really six parts to the actual healthcare component of a health plan. Let's take a look at each one individually, briefly describe it's purpose and then discuss how it would be covered under a cost-sharing plan (at participating providers) and also discuss how likely the relative services covered within each component are utilized.

- Doctor Visits—coverage for either primary care or specialty care office visits will continue to be covered subject to an office co-pay. Obviously, these charges are likely to happen to a broad scope of consumers.

- Labwork and Minor Radiological Testing—coverage for blood work, laboratory testing and x-rays will continue to be covered subject to the in-network co-pay. Charges for these services are also fairly likely to occur.

- Prescription Drugs—coverage for generic and brand-name drugs will continue to be subject to co-payments under the chosen prescription drug card. As we all know and have discussed, charges relative to this component will occur.

- Major Radiological Testing—coverage for MRIs, PET Scant CT Scans and more involved nuclear medicine will be subject to an in-network deductible, coinsurance and maximum out-of-pocket. Charges for these services are not very likely to occur for all covered employees and dependents.

- Outpatient Surgeries—coverage for procedures and surgeries performed outside the scope of a standard office visit. These charges are also not likely to occur for all employees and are therefore also subject to an in-network deductible, coinsurance and maximum out-of-pocket.

- Inpatient Hospitalizations—coverage for hospitalization greater than 23 hours in length of stay. Studies have repeatedly shown only 8%-12% of insured consumers will undergo an inpatient hospitalization in a given year. Given the averages, charges for these services will be subject to an in-network deductible, coinsurance and maximum out-of-pocket.

As you can see the goal of this health insurance program is to provide a stepping-stone towards consumer directed healthcare. It removes some, not all, of the first dollar benefits associated with a typical managed care plan. It lessens the coverage by placing a deductible, coinsurance and maximum out of pocket on the least likely of medical services. This serves to put some "employee skin in the game" and also generates a premium savings of often 10%-25%, depending of the degree of cost sharing implemented. In others words, the higher the deductible and maximum out-of-pocket you choose, the greater the premium savings that will be generated.

4.2 Deductible-First Health Insurance

(aka High Deductible Health Plans or HDHPs)

Deductible-first plans are just that, the deductible precedes reimbursement for all charges, prescription drugs included, before the insurance company provides reimbursement for eligible medical expenses. Upon their establishment by the Treasury Department in 2002, the minimum deductible was $1,000 per individual and $2,000 per family up until 2006 when it began indexing or increasing in accordance with inflation. Currently in 2007, the minimum deductible amount is $1,100 individual / $2,200 family and the maximum out-of-pocket limit is $5,500 individual / $11,000 family.

Standard managed care benefits would resume subsequent to satisfying the deductible. Typical Deductible-First Health Insurance or a High Deductible Health Plan would look like this:

Deductible-First Health Insurance
(example – PPO or POS based)

In-Network	Out-of-Network	Prescription Card
100% Coverage	70% Coverage	$10/$25/$50
High Deductible ($1,100 to $5,500)		

A Deductible-first health program encompassing the minimum deductible as defined by law is a pre-requisite and a requirement in order for an employee to maintain a Health Savings Account. Deductible-first health insurance programs can also be utilized with an Health Reimbursement Arrangement or if specific criteria are met, in conjunction with both an HSA and an HRA.

4.3 The Two Kinds of Deductibles

(Deductible-First Health Insurance or HDHPs)

Deductibles come in two forms, the aggregate and the embedded. Both have their pros and cons so let's walk through a deductible first health insurance program with a deductible of $2,500 employee only / $5,000 employee and dependents. Keep in mind, under either definition, the employee only deductible would be $2,500. Whether a deductible is aggregate or embedded only matters to those with employee and dependents coverage.

An aggregate deductible means all family members must collectively meet (in any formula possible) the collective or aggregate deductible of $5,000 before any one family member is eligible for covered expenses reimbursement. This will not be the preferred method for those electing dependent coverage with only one unhealthy family member. In that scenario, the one ill family member may need to satisfy the majority, if not all, of the deductible before reimbursement begins.

An embedded deductible means that a lower "individual only" deductible has been embedded into the aggregate deductible. Keeping with our example of a $5,000 deductible, the embedded or individual deductible would be $2,500. That would mean that one unhealthy family member would only have to meet

$2,500 in deductible before reimbursement would begin. The embedded deductible method is a newer sounding term for the method of deductible application used by the majority of health plans out there in the marketplace today.

4.4 It's All About The MOOP

As we discussed, back in the day we used to ask ourselves, "what's the deductible?" and "what's the maximum out-of-pocket?" when evaluating health insurance. Managed care has trained to ask, "what's the co-pay" as we became consumed with first-dollar benefits. We are now back to the original questions and concerning ourselves, for purposes of comparison, with the deductible amount and the maximum out-of-pocket.

Deductible first health insurance will generate a significant premium savings (as much as 40%-50%) over the costs of a traditional managed care plan. We will need to weigh the premium savings generated versus the increased up-front and total liability (the deductible and MOOP, respectively) and make an educated decision going forward. That liability will also enter into several considerations as we move into the other products we will discuss in this section as well as Section Five—The Roadmap.

4.5 Health Reimbursement Arrangements (HRAs)

This is an employer tool established by the Treasury's HRA Regulations of 2002. This is a regulation that allows employers to budget a calculated amount of benefit dollars and place them in an account so employees can use them for current or future claims as long as they remained insured by the underlying health insurance or health plan. It is meant to distinguish itself as 100% employer money as opposed to the commingled employer and employee funds that may be placed in a Flexible Spending Account (FSA). Employees are not permitted to contribute to an HRA.

This is a method for an employer to self-fund certain medical expenses or a certain dollar amount of claims per employee. The employer can decide which very specific medical expenses the HRA will reimburse. For example, the expenses subject to deductible and coinsurance under a cost sharing plan. For another, the HRA could reimburse all or a portion of the deductible in a deductible-first program. Below is the example of how an HRA might be used in conjunction with a cost sharing plan:

	Cost Sharing Plan (example – PPO or POS based)		
	In-Network	Out-of-Network	Prescription Card
Health Reimbursement Arrangement	100% Coverage	70% Coverage	$10/$25/$50
Employer Funded	Deductible & Coinsurance	Deductible	

Health Reimbursement Arrangements are notional accounts and in most instances, they are not pre-funded. The employer would fund the account at the point in which claims are incurred. Employers decide if unused balances carry forward to the following year, carry over in-part, carry over in accordance with a schedule based on years of service (for example) or do not carry over at all. They are not portable as they are employer owned. However, HRAs are considered to be part of a group health insurance program and must be made available to COBRA participants.

4.6 Flexible Spending Accounts (FSAs)

The addition of a flexible spending account provides an annual method of allowing employees to use pre-tax dollars to pay for unreimbursed medical expenses such as deductible co-pays and a laundry list of other items (we'll provide in the full list in an upcoming section). Pre-tax is defined as money being deducted from the consumer's gross income rather than the after-tax, net income. An employee savings of approximately 30% is gained by using wages that have not been subjected to Federal Income Tax, State Income Tax (except in NJ) and Social Security/Medicare taxes.

The employer can decide to limit the scope of eligible expenses. For example, flexible spending accounts can be used solely for reimbursement of dental and vision expenses in lieu of offering group coverage. The employer also determines the maximum amount an employee can contribute annual to his or her account. Employers also save money in this process due to the fact that employees' collective contributions lowers the employer's payroll and generates significant tax savings as a result.

Employee contributions to a flexible spending account must be used by the end of the plan year or by the end of the employer defined grace period for that same plan year. This is often referred to as the "use-it or lose-it" provision. Employees can access the account's funds by the submission of a manual claim or more commonly through the use of a debit card. Flexible spending accounts by nature, promote consumer budgeting for medical expenses, a concept critical to the success of consumer directed healthcare.

It is important to note that flexible spending accounts are a universally useful product. From the healthy to the chronically ill and from the wealthy to those living paycheck to paycheck, we all have medical expenses ranging from negligible to major. A flexible spending account is a universal way to save 30% on your medical services regardless of the underlying amount.

4.7 Medical Expense Budgeting

The vast majority of healthcare consumers do not budget for medical expenses. As we previously mentioned, nearly half of all insured consumers budget $1,000 or less for medical care and a surprising number of them do not budget anything at all. We budget for food, housing expenses, vacations, and new cars but not for medical care. Well, we are a result of the behavior that managed care has instilled in all of us. At the inception of managed care, co-payments were so low and first dollar benefits were so robust that we did not really need to budget—we essentially had a true 100% coverage. But again, the text of this book serves to provide and illustrate a better way. To better exemplify what should become the standard for the healthcare consumer in all of us, let's take a look at Jeffrey's father in law (bet you didn't see that coming?).

His father in law is a 68 year old man and is as pleasant as can be. He does not now, nor has he ever maintained a credit card, a debit card or even a checking account. He has never written a check. He replaces previous and current technology and the financial standards society has thrust upon us, with about twenty or so #10 size, white envelopes (the perfect size for dollar bills). The old adage "it's not what you make, it's how much you keep" was probably coined by someone who knew him and how he has successfully budgeted for anything and everything he or his family has ever wanted or needed using the "envelope method".

We need to develop a method for budgeting for medical care. As more pricing information becomes available every day, we need to utilize that information to develop an educated snapshot of the total cost of medical care we can reasonably expect to have for an upcoming block of time, typically a year What prescriptions do you take? How many times do you typically visit your primary care physician? How many times do you visit specialists for follow-up care? Add those charges up, subtract your assumed reimbursement under your medical plan and then add, once again, the costs of the over-the-counter or non-covered charges you can expect to incur and then budget for the total amount. This amount should be contributed pre-tax to the aforementioned flexible spending account or our next topic of discussion.

4.8 Health Savings Accounts (HSAs)

Deductible-First Health Insurance
(example – PPO or POS based)

Health Savings Account	In-Network	Out-of-Network	Prescription Card
	100% Coverage	70% Coverage	$10/$25/$50
Pre-Tax Money	High Deductible ($1,100 to $5,000)		

A lot of people think Health Savings Accounts or HSAs are synonymous with consumer directed healthcare, sort of the way Kleenex is synonymous with tissues. They are not but they are closely linked. Consumer directed healthcare is a movement or concept to give power to the patient and HSAs are a tool to utilize that power. In order to contribute and withdraw from a health savings account, the consumer must be enrolled in the previously defined deductible-first or high deductible health plan. The HSA account holder must not be covered for first-dollar benefits by any medical insurance program or plan through any employer or via a spouse's plan.

Health Savings Accounts, by the boring definition in other books (certainly not as entertaining as this one!), are tax advantaged accounts defined by IRS Code Section 213d and established by the Medicare Prescription Drug Improvement and Modernization Act of 2003. That's useless information, huh? That's why we were tempted to skip the background altogether.

Employees covered by the more appropriate and controlled deductible-first, health insurance plans can contribute pre-tax dollars (as previously defined in the FSA section) to this account to do one of two moves—(1) pay for the deductible and other medical expenses; we'll get to the full-list of eligible items in a few pages or (2) save the money for future medical expenses or retirement.

So who can contribute? Anybody can contribute to the eligible consumer's HSA on his or her behalf. The employer can make a contribution and save on the Income tax, Social Security, Medicare and Unemployment taxes, the employee can make contributions via payroll deduction and save on Federal/State Income Tax, Social Security and Medicare taxes or anyone at all can make an after-tax contribution at any time. In other words, these can be funded by whomever at any time.

As with anything good, there are limits. The maximum amount in 2007 a consumer can contribute annually to an HSA is $2,850 individual/$5,650 family. The aforementioned limits assume a calendar year from January 1st through December 31st. If an HSA in established mid-year, the maximum contributions used to be pro-rated; however given late 2006 legislation, the full limit amounts can still be contributed. As we mentioned, monies deposited in the account grow tax—deferred and are withdrawn for eligible medical expenses tax-free. The only time funds would be taxed is if you (a) deposited too much in a given year or (b) you withdraw funds for non-eligible expenses such as plasma televisions or Jimmy Choo shoes. We might think they are medically necessary to our happiness but the IRS does not share our sense of humor.

Health savings accounts are employee-owned. Any and all funds deposited by the employee and/or the employer are fully vested and are the employee's from day one. The accounts are portable from one employer to the next. Accounts are set up through a bank or financial institution and can be either facilitated by the insurer providing the deductible-first medical insurance program or they can be completely independent and provided separately.

Unlike flexible spending accounts there is no "use-it or lose-it" rule, no grace period or time frame in which the funds must be utilized or spent down. Funds roll over from year to year, which leads us to our next topic …

4.9 Remember the Now and Later?

Remember that hard, square shaped candy with the wrapper that was impossible to remove? The one on which our mother always claimed we would choke? Health spending accounts are much like the candy in that consumers can use them now, use them later or a combination of both. This dispels the myth that HSAs are just for the healthy and wealthy. It is true that HSAs to some degree may divide consumers into two categories: "savers" and "spenders". The savers may very well be comprised of the healthy and wealthy. The spenders may be those not in a position to save based upon earnings or those with active medical concerns and current or ongoing treatment needs. Either way, on either side of the line in the sand, there are positives to both approaches.

The "savers" or those in a position either by virtue of good health or fortune may not need to access to the pre-tax funds deposited into their accounts. The account can become a savings vehicle should medical concerns present in the future or as a vehicle to enhance the retirement savings we all should be concerned about regardless of age. Again, this account when controlled by a "saver", functions much like an IRA or Individual Retirement Account. Employers reap the benefit of a lowered payroll as employee contributions to an HSA reduces taxable income much like 401k contributions.

The "spenders" are those who are not in a position to save these pre-tax funds and must use them to reimburse medical expenses based upon income or health. For them, health savings accounts function much like an ATM machine and a relative account. They can now access funds to reimburse deductibles, co-payments, qualified medical expenses, COBRA premiums, and the other items on the list we keep promising will follow at the end of this section. They may never be able to take advantage of the savings aspect of an HSA but they will continually be able to take advantage of the significant savings associated with enrolling in a deductible-first health insurance program and paying for that deductible with pre-tax dollars.

4.10 Wellness Programs and Health Incentive Accounts (HIAs)

A well-publicized wellness program that incents employees to become actively engaged in their own health and well-being is critical to the success of consumer directed healthcare. Simply put, wellness programs make sure the Healthy and Well stay on track, lead the Unhealthy but Well on the road to a healthy lifestyle and make sure the Chronically Ill are educated as to the resources available to them.

Most wellness programs begin with a health assessment questionnaire that forces participants to analyze their family health history, nutrition, physical activity and stress levels. Then participants undergo an individual, on-site screening where typical physical exam type tests and laboratory screenings are performed. This is followed by an personalized consultation where the test results are discussed, high risk behaviors or medical evidence is discussed, wellness goals are set and positive lifestyle behaviors and recognized, set in motion or reinforced.

Wellness programs typically target preventable, chronic illness and set their focus in four main areas of concern: cholesterol, blood sugar, blood pressure and weight management. Members who exhibit pre-chronic symptoms or evidence are provided educational resources and tools t help them develop and maintain the healthy lifestyle changes required in order to diminish or eliminate the pre-chronic symptoms.

Participants are also provided constant communication and access to tools and resources all for the purpose of maintaining a healthy lifestyle. Newsletters, periodic on-site presentations, payroll stuffers and on-line tools are all promoted heavily and often. After all, wellness is a never-ending process not an event.

Employers can receive aggregate reporting as to the company's performance. Reporting is done on a global basis as to confirm to the legislation concerning patient privacy.

Many employers have chosen to tie employees' participation to a Health Incentive Account. These are accounts that can reward participation and ongoing effort in several ways. Some HIAs feature participants accumulating points for either cash rewards or prizes. Others allow participants the access to additional employer funds provided via an HRA or the most common, a lower employee contribution cost to the medical plan.

4.11 Ok, Ok—Here's The List

The long awaited list is here. The list of eligible medical service for which consumers can use their pre-tax dollars accumulated in a Health Savings Account to reimburse. In retrospect, we kind of teased this like that big news story they only give us half the information about until the news actually airs at 11 PM. Sorry. Anyway, here it is:

Deductible Medical Expenses			Nondeductible Medical Expenses
• Abdominal supports	• Drugs *(prescription)*	• Osteopath	• Advancement payment for services to be rendered next year
• Abortion	• Elastic hosiery *(prescription)*	• Oxygen and oxygen equipment	• Athletic Club membership
• Acupuncture	• Eyeglasses	• Pediatrician	• Automobile insurance premium allocable to medical coverage
• Air conditioner *(when necessary for relief from difficulty in breathing)*	• Fees paid to health institute prescribed by a doctor	• Physician	• Boarding school fees
• Alcoholism treatment	• FICA and FUTA tax paid for medical care service	• Physiotherapist	• Bottled Water
• Ambulance	• Fluoridation unit	• Podiatrist	• Commuting expenses of a disabled person
• Anesthetist	• Guide dog	• Postnatal treatments	• Cosmetic surgery and procedures
• Arch supports	• Gum treatment	• Practical nurse for medical services	• Cosmetics, hygiene products and similar items
• Artificial limbs	• Gynecologist	• Prenatal care	• Diaper service
• Autoette *(when used for relief of sickness/disability)*	• Healing services	• Prescription medicines	• Domestic help
• Birth Control Pills *(by prescription)*	• Hearing aids and batteries	• Psychiatrist	• Funeral, cremation, or burial expenses
• Blood tests	• Hospital bills	• Psychoanalyst	• Health programs offered by resort hotels, health clubs, and gyms
• Blood transfusions	• Hydrotherapy	• Psychologist	• Illegal operations and treatments
• Braces	• Insulin treatment	• Psychotherapy	• Illegally procured drugs
• Cardiographs	• Lab tests	• Radium Therapy	• Maternity clothes
• Chiropractor	• Lead paint removal	• Registered nurse	• Non-prescription medication
• Childbirth/Delivery	• Legal fees	• Special school costs for the handicapped	• Premiums for life insurance, income protection, disability, loss of limbs, sight or similar benefits
• Christian Science Practitioner	• Lodging *(away from home for outpatient care)*	• Spinal fluid test	• Scientology counseling
• Contact Lenses	• Metabolism tests	• Splints	• Social activities
• Contraceptive devices *(by prescription)*	• Neurologist	• Sterilization	• Special foods and beverages
• Convalescent home *(for medical treatment only)*	• Nursing *(including board and meals)*	• Surgeon	• Specially designed car for the handicapped other than an autoette or special equipment
• Crutches	• Obstetrician	• Telephone or TV equipment to assist the hard-of-hearing	• Stop-smoking programs
• Dental Treatment	• Operating room costs	• Therapy equipment	• Swimming pool
• Dental X-rays	• Ophthalmologist	• Transportation expenses *(relative to health care)*	• Travel for general health improvement
• Dentures	• Optician	• Ultra-violet ray treatment	• Tuition and travel expenses a problem child to a particular school
• Dermatologist	• Optometrist	• Vaccines	• Weight loss programs
• Diagnostic fees	• Oral surgery	• Vasectomy	
• Diathermy	• Organ transplant *(including donor's expenses)*	• Vitamins *(if prescribed)*	
• Drug addiction therapy	• Orthopedic shoes	• Wheelchair	
	• Orthopedist	• X-rays	

Part Five

The Roadmap

5.1 This Is Not The Equivalent Of The Pet Rock

Still think this is a fad? Think this will come and go? We urge you to think again. Wellpoint, the nation's largest benefits provider, has vowed that they will make consumer directed health insurance available to individuals, small groups and large groups in all fifty states. Consumer directed healthcare is gaining popularity and acceptance on a far larger and faster scale than managed care did. To compete, insurance companies (who are mostly publicly traded—hint, hint) will be reducing premiums by offering and selling mostly deductible-first insurance. They will also be investing heavily in consumer technology to keep pace for the demand for pricing, quality and wellness information. With Wall Street watching revenues dip and expenses spike, they are going to make certain this works!

"Inside Consumer Directed Care" is a newsletter published by Atlantic Information Systems and they produced a report in September, 2006. According to their report, 1.17 million Health Savings Accounts were established by financial firms such as JP Morgan and Wells Fargo. They contain upwards of 1.5 billion dollars in assets. These statistics increased by 50% from January 1, 2006. According to the United States Government Accountability Office's Consumer Directed Healthcare Report in April of 2006, the number of enrollees in deductible—first medical insurance plans, consumer directed health insurance doubled from three million to six million from January, 2005 to January, 2006. Additionally, three quarters of Fortune 500 companies will offer a consumer directed healthcare option by or in 2007.

Everyday insurers are building their position behind this movement. Carriers are making network pricing information and fee schedules available to their members. Medicare (the government's plan), who normally trail blazes new concepts, has also made fee schedules available to the public for the most popular procedures. Consumer tools are either being developed by the carriers or they are purchasing existing tools and technology and revolutionizing their functionality.

Literally as we write this passage, an article has come across our desks of an insurer that is beta-testing and finalizing revolutionary technology. They have developed technology to enable providers to electronically submit claims, have it re-priced according to network discounts, processed according to the consumer's benefit plan and instantaneously report back the member liability; all this with the swipe of a debit card.

Another national insurer has developed the technology allowing employees to maintain an all-in-one identification card. The identification card will function as proof of eligibility as it always had but it will also include added technology and functionality. The card will also act as the debit card providing the cardholder access to their HSA accounts to pay for medical services. Additionally, it will allow employees access to lines of credit equivalent to the amount of funds they intend to contribute to the account periodically by way of payroll deduction thruought the year. Lastly, the card will serve as a pass code to the consumers' medical and family history. Again, all this with the swipe of a card.

Lastly, a banking institution has teamed with a leading prescription vendor to offer reward points for joint consumers. Each time the card is used for a generic or preferred brand name drug versus the more, costly non-preferred drugs advertised on television, the consumer will receive reward points. Points are then redeemed for cash and prizes similar to most credit card programs.

The government endorses this movement, the insurance carriers and banking institutions are behind this movement, Fortune 500 companies are implementing this movement and technology supports this movement. That only leaves employers and medical providers to either drive off the road or brake with the ones that follow.

5.2 Welcome to Wherever You Are

So we've discussed the full scope of the problem. We've discussed the extent of the attitudes, perceptions and behaviors conducive to the solution. We've discussed the products that will help us regain a healthy medical insurance program. But like typical insurance brokers, we have not yet provided the answer. This section will provide the roadmap to get from wherever you are to where you need to be and offer you the option of taking a short cut or the scenic route.

According to Great West Healthcare, we need to look before we leap. Before launching head first into consumer directed healthcare like Super Dave being shot out of a canyon, we need to take the pulse of our objectives as employers and the compatibility of our employees. We need to examine:

- Long Term Plan Objectives. A one-year strategy does not cut it anymore. We need to know what we want Year Three to look like to enable us to properly design the benefit programs in Year One and Year Two.

- Employee Readiness. Employers will need to rev' up their staff. They need to educate and over-communicate the problems with managed care and the paradigm shift necessary to create an environment and a willingness to adopt the proposed solutions.

- Determine What Works. How can the employer create and stimulate the attitudes necessary to cultivate an acceptance of consumerism and deflate the entitlement mentality that is certainly embedded at this point. This may translate to lessened employee contributions, employer-funding of HSA programs or the limiting of options in the years to come. Employers need to determine what action or actions will both spark the changes necessary while gaining the most positive reaction from employees possible.

- Multiple Options. Employers need to create options just like consumer directed healthcare intends to do. Often times, positive employee word-of-mouth is the most powerful tool in the employer's toolbox. Medical insurance offerings can be structured in a way to garner a pre-determined outcome.

- Commitment To Education. Trial by fire and "let's see how it goes" are not strategies. According to Dave Marcum and Steve Smith in their book, Business Think, "Hope is not a strategy." Employers need to be committed to ongoing education and over-communication in order for the shift in the consumers' or employees' mindsets to be achieved.

- Commitment To Improved Health. Consumer directed healthcare is not about a change in plan design. As this text hopefully successfully conveyed, it is about a whole lot more than that. Wellness and the commitment on the part of both employers and employees to wage a war against our ambivalence to leading an unhealthy lifestyle is paramount. As Jeffrey Gitomer, Sales Guru, often says, "we need to be committed to change and remain committed to our commitment."

The section will have to make some assumptions concerning where you are at the moment in order to provide direction as to where to go and how to get there. Hopefully, we'll cover all the bases and provide guidelines and several ideas that can be implemented tomorrow or at renewal to get the benefits program moving in the right direction now or to set the stage for the future.

5.3 The Natural Evolution

Generally speaking, most employers move through the food chain of managed care to consumer directed healthcare in this fashion. This should be the roadmap when the scenic route is taken and the progression is performed incrementally. This evolution can also certainly endorse the idea of running with one leg and dragging the other. What does that mean? It means employers can both continue to offer previous step's programs (managed care) and diminish their availability year by year, always gravitating towards consumer directed healthcare but at an employer defined pace.

The first step of the progression begins with a single employer-sponsored program and then moves incrementally through the other four steps concluding with full blown consumer directed healthcare—deductible-first health insurance with a Health Savings Account.

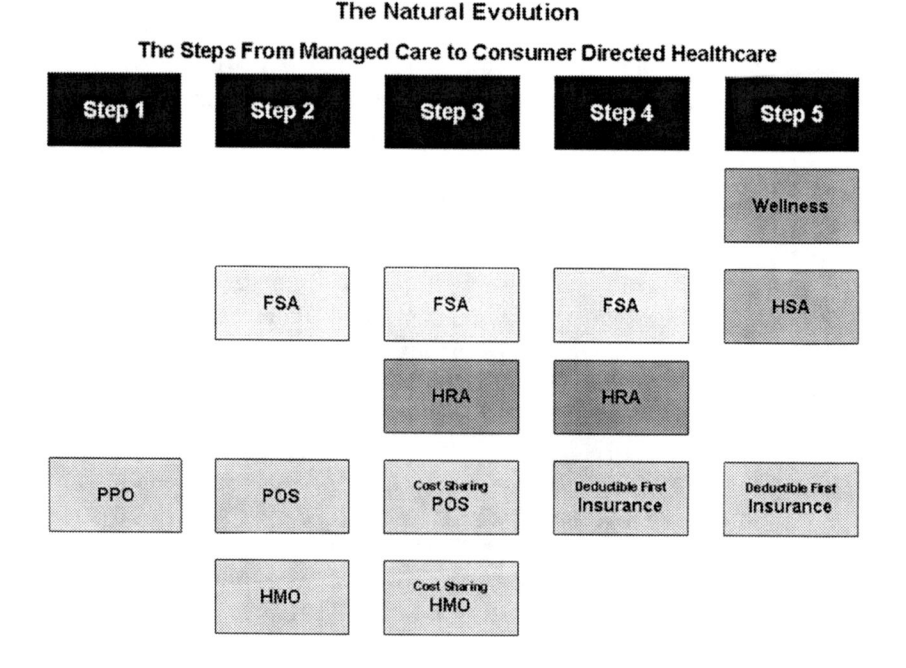

The Natural Evolution
The Steps From Managed Care to Consumer Directed Healthcare

Step 1	Step 2	Step 3	Step 4	Step 5
				Wellness
	FSA	FSA	FSA	HSA
		HRA	HRA	
PPO	POS	Cost Sharing POS	Deductible First Insurance	Deductible First Insurance
	HMO	Cost Sharing HMO		

Step One is a single employer sponsored health plan. Employees participate in the plan or they do not. Often, the plan is not coupled with a medical budgeting or savings mechanism such as an FSA. This does not promote the advantages of consumerism and does not allow employees to select from a myriad of plans.

Step Two is (you guessed it!) a step in the right direction. This program is typically a dual option offering meaning employees can select from one of two medical plan options depending upon their healthcare needs and the amount they wish to contribute to the plan's cost. These programs are generally coupled with an FSA, a building block to begin the education and implementation of a budgeting process for employees.

Step Three is the initial step of consumer directed healthcare. Under this scenario, the employer would continue to offer a dual-option offering whereby employees can select the plan design of which they are most comfortable with according to the relative benefits and cost. The plan offerings would incorporate an element of cost-sharing which would create an increased out-of-pocket for the participating employees. Often times, that increased liability would be partially self-funded and reimbursed through an employer sponsored HRA. Continuing the education and advancement of employees' awareness of the cost of medical care and how to effectively engrain a method for budgeting for medical care, an FSA is still offered.

Step Four is an advancement of the consumer directed healthcare movement. Under this scenario, the employer offers a single deductible-first heath insurance program but provides the opportunity to participate in several levels of employer HRA contribution (used to reimburse the deductible) by establishing two or three levels of employee contributions. For example, let's assume the deductible-first program had a $1,500 deductible. The employee who does not wish to take advantage of the HRA might have a $0 or minimal contribution to the program. An employee who wishes to take advantage of a $1,000 employer HRA contribution might contribute $80 per month to the program. Employees are still encouraged to contribute to and utilize an FSA.

Step Five is synonymous with full commitment. It is deductible-first health insurance coupled with both an HSA and a wellness program. This step incorporates all the aspects of consumer directed healthcare. An FSA is no longer needed as the employees can now contribute to their individually owned Health Savings Accounts. Employers may still choose to offer various levels of employee contribution to the program in order to share in the premium cost or in exchange for an employer sponsored contribution to the employee owned HSAs. A wellness program is also offered and is best operated with a employee contribution discount or additional employer HSA contribution as an incentive for employees who participate and complete the program's suggested steps to a health lifestyle.

For example, smokers who quit smoking will only pay $75 per month as an employee contribution versus the standard $90 per month.

5.4 The Road To Somewhere

Here's how consumer directed healthcare normally plays out. If you agree we should stop buying health plans and start buying health insurance, this is the incremental roadmap to follow. Employers do not need to wait until the market thrusts a move upon your healthcare (like it already hasn't!). Here are the proactive steps to take now to build a properly functioning, healthy and controlled medical care program for the future.

Ever watched a movie and thought to yourself? Wow!, that scene was utterly uselsss; I'll never get that ten minutes back! If you have thought that, think again. Every scene in a movie serves to carry the story along even if it only inches a very bad movie or story forward. Think about what is involved in filming a scene? There are lights that need to be set up and set up in a fashion that matches previous scenes that were shot or adjusts the time day to make it look like it is later or earlier in the day. Audio needs to be recorded, actors need to be positioned, shots need to filmed, takes need to be done. All this effort can amount to hours or days of work to sometimes get two minutes of film.

Employers should think of their health insurance offering the same way movies are made. Do not make an uncalculated move. Design how your health insurance offering will look like in the future and then make the incremental steps necessary to get it down that path to the destination. Changing the slighest benefit or altering employee contributions in the most nominal of ways should all be done with the end goal in mind. Every time a health insurance program is altered, it should be done to move the program along to what you decided it needed to look like. Just like a scene to a movie or an integral part of your business plan.

These steps are designed to be a logical path to implement full-blown consumer directed healthcare in a four year time period. It assumes your company currently maintains some semblance of a managed care offering currently.

The Road To Somewhere
The Incremental Progression of Consumer Directed Healthcare

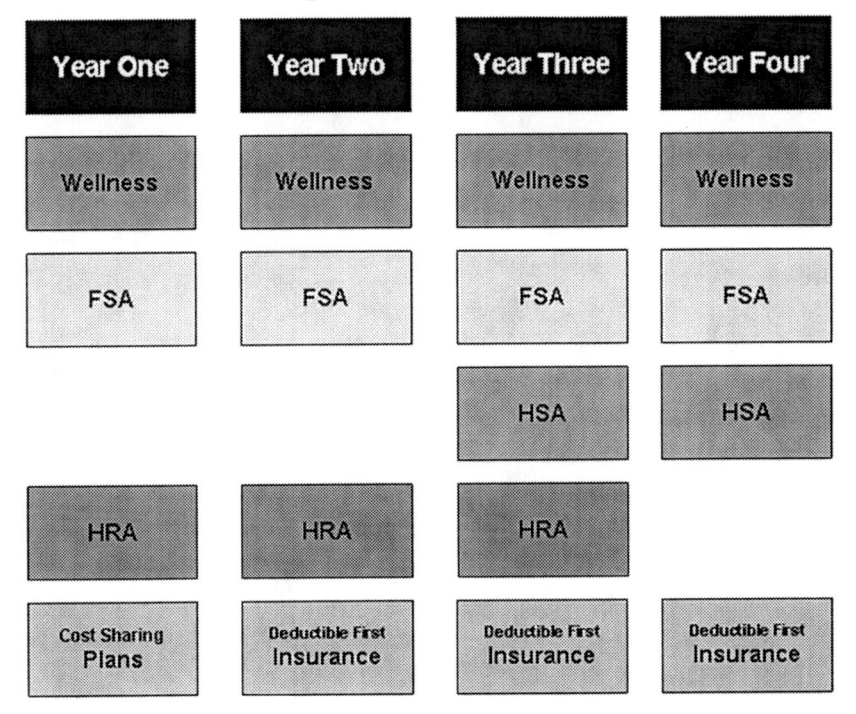

Year One	Year Two	Year Three	Year Four
Wellness	Wellness	Wellness	Wellness
FSA	FSA	FSA	FSA
		HSA	HSA
HRA	HRA	HRA	
Cost Sharing Plans	Deductible First Insurance	Deductible First Insurance	Deductible First Insurance

Year One should include the altering of your current managed care offering to a cost-sharing plan. If you recall from Section Four—4.1 Cost Sharing Plans, these plans remove the 100% coverage from the medical services least likely to be rendered. That way the employer can install an HRA and fund it with the dollars saved to reimburse employees some or all of the additional liability created by the cost-sharing plan. It's a safe and calculated bet. It's a big bet but with pocket aces, it's self-funding but with training wheels. The guarantee is that the premium will be reduced; the variable is the amount of money that will actually be utilized from the HRA. Any insurance professional can tell you, this will work out year after year to your advantage.

Employers will want to include an FSA to once again promote medical budgeting and the use of pre-tax dollars to reimburse unpaid medical expenses. A wellness plan will also act as a nice accompaniment to promote healthy lifestyles amongst your employees.

Year Two will bring the arrival of the deductible-first health insurance program. At this point, employer education and communication of the values associated with consumer directed healthcare will be in full force. However, Year Two will still assume some help from the employer once again in the form of an HRA. Employers can seek a program that incorporates the minimum deductible allowed by the incremental schedule the government produced ($1,100 in 2007). Employers will fund some or all of the deductible, employees will watch on the sidelines until it's their turn to put their money in the game. They will see firsthand how the program works and how it will function for them in years to come. They'll begin to become involved in cost considerations as they will have to consciously pay for medical services until the deductible is satisfied (albeit with the employer's money).

Once again, employers should strongly promote the use of both an FSA and a wellness plan. Their understanding and usage will be paramount in the years to come when consumer directed healthcare is in full swing and only employee money is at stake.

Year Three will once again utilize a deductible-first health insurance program but this time the deductible will be higher than the government dictated minimum (again $1,100 in 2007 so let's assume for our example, we choose a $1,500 deductible). This is where the medical budgeting skills, know-how and interest that was promoted and cultivated in previous years will pay off for those employees who chose to be engaged in your foresight. Employees will be on their own for the minimum deductible and will be prompted to fund the minimum deductible amount, not through an FSA, but an HSA, a Health Spending Account. The employer HRA will be funded to financially accommodate employees the difference between the government dictated minimum deductible and the actual deductible amount of the deductible-first health insurance program you chose to implement.

The FSA will remain but will now be limited in use. It will be limited to non-medical expenses and expenses not covered by the medical plan. The wellness plan is now ever-so-important as employees are playing the game with their own dollars and a financial stake in maintaining a healthy lifestyle to eliminate health care cost altogether.

At this point, employers should have led employees up the stairs one-by-one and thereby created a staff of wise healthcare consumers who have re-cultivated an awareness and consideration for both cost and quality of care. At this point, employees in general and employees with health conditions should have developed a sense of value and appreciation for their employer-sponsored healthcare offering.

Year Four is full-blown consumer directed healthcare. Employees are on their own and the employer's wallet is no longer a leather bound ATM machine so to speak. Employers should choose to keep the deductible level the same as Year Three as it can be increased in years to come as the consumer directed healthcare programs becomes the norm and employees begin to fully appreciate the value of an HSA. The HRA is gone and the HSA coupled with the limited use FSA remain as a way for employees to budget for medical care expenses both during the deductible accumulation and subsequent once the insurance reimbursement begins and the managed care benefits resume.

Employers can continue to help employees by virtue of making a contribution to the employees' HSAs. Only now this is not a notional concept as the money becomes the employees as of Day One. It almost resembles a parting gift of sorts or one last head-start for the staff. Like never before, employees should take advantage of the wellness program. Employers can actually incent employees to participate and get the last of the nay-sayers engaged by offering an enhanced employer HSA contribution for those who participate.

This section served to offer a roadmap should you agree we should stop buying health plans and start buying health insurance. It is also not to assume employers have to abandon the thought of leaving one foot on the managed care side and one foot on the consumer directed healthcare side. There are many variations within the roadmap to accomplish the same end-game. The next four sections will enhance upon the premise that you agree (to some extent) with the roadmap you've just been handed and the destination you've just been promised.

5.5 We Don't Need No Uneducated Consumer (No Employee Left Behind)

However long or short the rev-up process is, employees will still have concern. It's what they do. Employers must rely on proactive education and continuous over-communication in order to separate the static consumer directed healthcare will initially create. The subgroup of most concern should be those who have chronic conditions and serious medical concern whom will require some additional and warranted hand-holding and a more personalized walk-through, so to speak.

Pre-education is the key to success in any change, in any paradigm shift. Healthcare success must be held up and visualized before it can be achieved.

Without a clear vision of the road ahead, employees will just be bowling in the dark and will become frustrated, annoyed and confused. When implementing your defined Step One, Step Two should also be explained during the renewal and implementation process and thruought the year by virtue of a "postcards and paychecks" system, in-house webinars, intranet education and periodic newsletters. Any good broker should have a system whereby they periodically produce value-first newsletters—one tailored for employers and the other for employees to "drip" healthcare education year round.

Get the gripes out of the way. Find out your employees concerns with your next step in advance of it's implementation. By doing so, you'll spend more time on your healthcare plan but you will also have sufficient time to either alter your chosen Step Two, to accommodate forecasted concerns or tailor an education process to remedy them. Again, employees should know what your plan design intentions are prior to implementation so they have the opportunity to become accustomed to the behavioral or financial changes future plan design choices will generate. After all, a mind changed against its will is of the same mind still.

As you will note, a wellness program is a staple in the steps of our outlined plans of implementing a consumer directed healthcare program or offering. Wellness plans will engage employees in the primary concepts of consumer directed healthcare and will lay a continuous foundation for employees to take responsibility for their health. Wellness programs also breed Health Incentive Accounts which reward participation and completion of the individualized actions required to live a healthy lifestyle.

The promotion of consumer tools before they are absolutely necessary is also paramount in consumer directed healthcare's implementation success. Employees should be constantly reminded of the availability of generic drugs and the financial benefits to consider their use. Many prescription drug card vendors currently maintain programs that will electronically notify employees via email of the generic equivalents each and every time they fill a brand-name drug prescription. Find out if your current vendor offers such a program and have the employees sign up.

Many carriers have also made their network contracted fee schedules available to their insureds on their member portal of their respective websites. This is access to information for both their managed care and consumer directed healthcare members. Before they are educated to the point of being active healthcare consumers, employees should be aware of these tools and their uses. They need to be educated as to how to obtain information about quality and price. For example, members in Southern Florida should know that one orthopedic surgeon is paid $1,713 for a hip replacement while a surgeon in the same town receives $1,456. Cincinnati members should be aware that one provider receives $127.62 for a new patient office visit while another provider in the same town receives $108.00. Employees should also be required or strongly encouraged to register for access to your current carrier's member portal.

The encouragement and education as to this information's use and availability is paramount to rev up towards implementing consumer directed healthcare in the proper, most positive environment possible.

5.6 Show Me The Money

All right already, here it is (well, almost). Again and before we get started detailing the above inserted chart, we need to remove the emotions associated with healthcare and de-humanize health insurance. We know it's personal and near and dear to us, but as we've stated it's a financial vehicle first and foremost. Managed care attempted to level the playing field for both the sick and the healthy by providing a equal level of benefit and an equal level of cost. Managed care can no longer do this and the sick should unfortunately pay more either in up-front costs (which is next to impossible to create a functional system to support this thought) or in the way of costs when medical services are rendered and the insurance is actually utilized. Keep this in mind as we discuss the chart.

The Premium Savings of Consumer Directed Healthcare

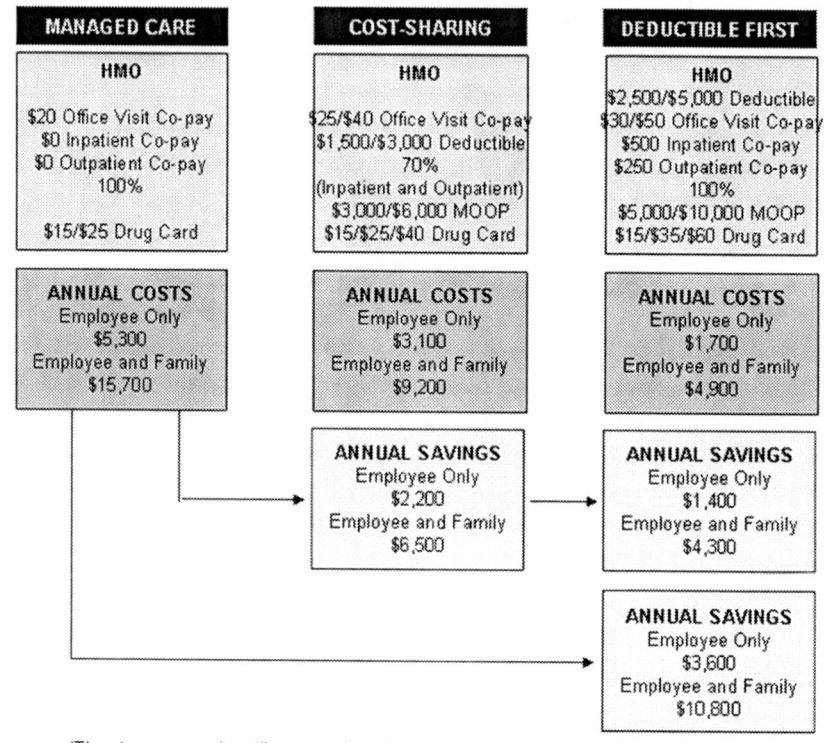

MANAGED CARE	COST-SHARING	DEDUCTIBLE FIRST
HMO	**HMO**	**HMO**
$20 Office Visit Co-pay	$25/$40 Office Visit Co-pay	$2,500/$5,000 Deductible
$0 Inpatient Co-pay	$1,500/$3,000 Deductible	$30/$50 Office Visit Co-pay
$0 Outpatient Co-pay	70%	$500 Inpatient Co-pay
100%	(Inpatient and Outpatient)	$250 Outpatient Co-pay
$15/$25 Drug Card	$3,000/$6,000 MOOP	100%
	$15/$25/$40 Drug Card	$5,000/$10,000 MOOP
		$15/$35/$60 Drug Card
ANNUAL COSTS	**ANNUAL COSTS**	**ANNUAL COSTS**
Employee Only	Employee Only	Employee Only
$5,300	$3,100	$1,700
Employee and Family	Employee and Family	Employee and Family
$15,700	$9,200	$4,900
	ANNUAL SAVINGS	**ANNUAL SAVINGS**
	Employee Only	Employee Only
	$2,200	$1,400
	Employee and Family	Employee and Family
	$6,500	$4,300
		ANNUAL SAVINGS
		Employee Only
		$3,600
		Employee and Family
		$10,800

(The above example utilizes a national insurer's rates for a sample NJ small employer.)

As you can see from even a quick glance, the premium dollars saved supports, at minimum, a significant portion of the additional liability—whether that be hypothetical liability in the form of cost sharing on specified services or up-front liability in a deductible-first program. This is important as there will need to be a financial upside to the employee in the form of one of the following in order to roll out a consumer directed game plan. The savings must support and be used to fund one of the following employee-perceived positives: lessened or eliminated employee contributions, HRA establishment to reimburse some or all of the additional liability or contributions to an employee's HSA.

In our above example, if an employer was to gravitate from the managed care plan to the cost-sharing program, those with employee only coverage will save $2,200 in annual premium. Now the office co-payments will be increased to a more consumer directed split co-payments of $25 for primary care and $40 for specialists. The prescription card will gravitate to a three-tier card to promote consumer awareness and the use of generic drugs by applying a more costly co-pay to the use of non-preferred brand-name drugs or the drugs you see advertised on television and in magazines. Other than those proposed, semi-negligible changes, the main difference is that outpatient and inpatient hospitalization use will be subject to a $1,500 annual deductible, a 70% co-insurance and a $3,000 maximum out of pocket. (It is important to note than in most plans, office co-payments, hospital co-payments and prescription card co-payments may be applied to the maximum out of pocket as well).

So we are talking about a definitive $2,200 in savings in exchange for an unlikely (certainly when this applied to a large group of insured employees) risk of $3,000. Even if employers, were to fund the full $2,200 through an HRA and every, single employee utilized inpatient and outpatient hospital-related services, the employer would still only break even. There would be no possibility of a financial downside. Taking a more realistic look, employers would win and win big as only 8-12% of insured employees will utilize these services.

In our above example, if an employer was to gravitate from the managed care plan to the deductible-first program, those with employee only coverage will save $3,600 in annual premium. Employers will realize a significant savings that will allow them to fund the full deductible (and beyond to include a portion of the co-payments) and utilize the plan as simply a deductible-first health insurance program. Employers can also choose to lessen the blow of the transition by allowing employees to establish an HSA and make a significant contribution to the account (the maximum contribution by any and all parties combined in our example would be $2,850 in 2007). Another option would be to allow employees to fund the minimum deductible allowed by law ($1,100 in 2007) and establish an HRA to fund the difference between the minimum deductible allowable by law and the actual deductible of the plan (or the difference between $1,100 and $2,500 if this took place in 2007).

As you can see, the money is there. Employers just need to know how to develop a consumer directed healthcare program that contrasts with their current managed care plan in such a way to generate sufficient enough savings to cover the additional liability cost-sharing and up-front deductibles create.

Now many of our critics will argue that the philosophies or strategies we outlined in this section as to how to utilize the premium savings will defeat the goals of consumer directed healthcare and will only serve to prolong the difficulties managed care created. We cannot argue this point nor do we agree that the savings should be used to fully fund deductibles and other liabilities in cost sharing and deductible first programs until the end of time. We took it to these extremes in our examples and analysis to make a point—the money is there in the way of premium savings. The savings is significant and warrants a change. How that change is implemented and how much the employer wants to fund will depend upon the up-front education employees can receive and the tolerance of typical employer groups to long term strategies requiring a shift in attitude and perception.

5.7 Fund, Fund, Fund 'Till Daddy Takes The T-Bird Away

Let's face it, there are two ways to skin this (healthcare) cat. Employers can choose to adopt consumer directed healthcare all at once or move employees in the direction incrementally like the lines at a Disney World attraction. From smaller employers like your local printer to mid-size companies like Whole Foods to large employers such as Pitney Bowes or Microsoft, there does not seem to be a steadfast set of protocols as to the best practice of how quickly to implement consumer directed healthcare.

The one constant if there is one is the presence of employer funding by establishing an HRA or employer contribution to an HSA. Helping employees along the path, eliminates, to some degree, the perception that consumer directed healthcare is a fancy new name for employers to keep the big bag of money at the end of the year. Putting your money where your mouth is creates a perception to the educated employee that consumer directed healthcare is the future, something to embrace and part of a long term strategy that is a "win-win-win" for employers, employees and medical providers alike.

The overly obvious concept of the employer's willingness to fund having a direct correlation to the amount of participation in an employer's consumer directed healthcare offering has been proven in countless surveys and reports. Before the advent of the television, the marketing tool used by most businesses to create a virus about a new product or concept was word-of-mouth. This concept is certainly one that will take off largely as the result of positive word of mouth. Current enrollees will do more to stimulate future enrollment than any other tool. Employees that are saving both premium dollars and pre-tax dollars in their HSA will have lots to talk about and talk they will.

It is obvious that we endorse the employer's leading by example and taking a proactive stance in this movement's progression. Just like managed care, it is up to brokers to educate employers as to the concept of consumer directed healthcare movement's ideals and tools. More importantly, it is up to employers to perpetuate the movement by purchasing and implementing the relative products conducive to the movement's progression. Lastly, it will be up to the employees and medical providers to engrain this concept as part of our everyday healthcare culture.

Chart 10 — Employer Health Benefits 2006 Annual Survey

Average Annual Premiums, Worker and Firm Contributions For Covered Workers in PPO and HDHP/SO Plans, 2006

	PPO		HDHP/SO	
	Single	Family	Single	Family
Worker Contribution to Premium	$637	$2,915*	$569	$2,247*
Firm Contribution to Premium	$3,749*	$8,850*	$2,836*	$7,238*
Total Annual Premium	$4,385*	$11,765*	$3,405*	$9,484*
Firm Contribution to the HRA or HSA	NA	NA	$743	$1,359
Total Annual Spending (Total Premium Plus Firm Contribution to HRA or HSA)	$4,385	$11,765	$4,148	$10,844

*Estimates are statistically different between PPO and HDHP/SO plans at p<.05.
NA: Not Applicable
Source: Kaiser/HRET Survey of Employer-Sponsored Health Benefits, 2006.

5.8 How To Set The Table

Employee contributions are very often an afterthought or the starting point in deciding how much of the increased cost of an employer's managed care plan employees will now be absorbing. Consumer directed healthcare changes the game or at minimum adds another arrow in the quiver of rewarding the proper employee perspective or creating a pre-determined outcome in employee plan selection. There are a million and one ways to structure an employee contribution schedule but we've outlined five. All adopt different philosophies but share one common goal—moving your organization down the road to consumer directed healthcare. For proposes of simplicity, we've chosen to use only HMO-based programs in each of the three offerings: the managed care plan, the cost-sharing plan and deductible-first insurance program.

Triple Option Scenario

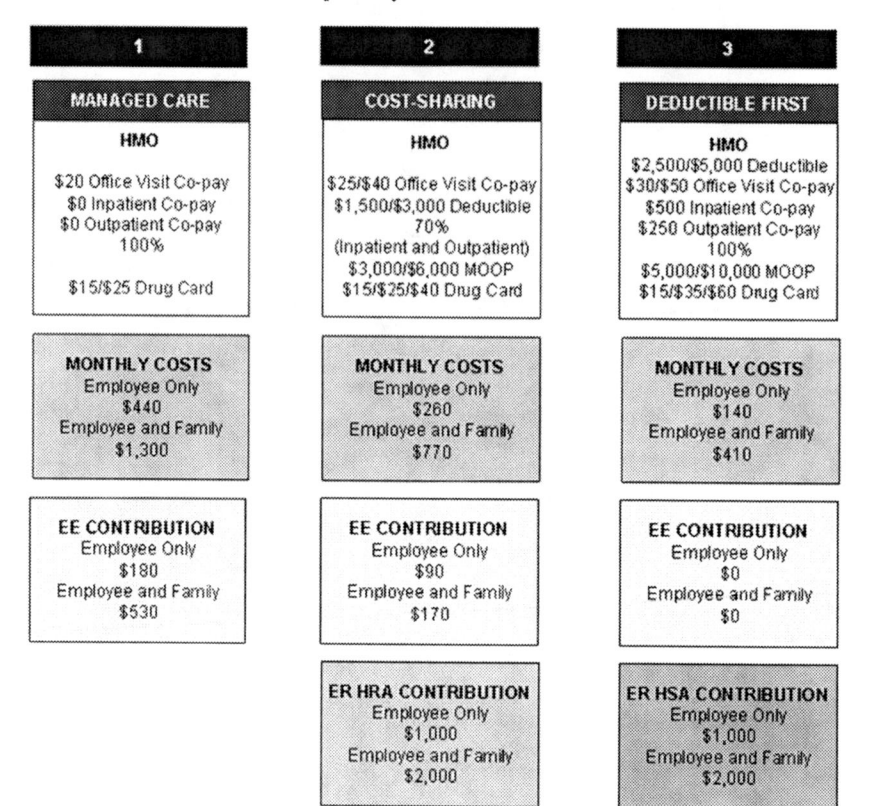

1 MANAGED CARE	2 COST-SHARING	3 DEDUCTIBLE FIRST
HMO $20 Office Visit Co-pay $0 Inpatient Co-pay $0 Outpatient Co-pay 100% $15/$25 Drug Card	**HMO** $25/$40 Office Visit Co-pay $1,500/$3,000 Deductible 70% (Inpatient and Outpatient) $3,000/$6,000 MOOP $15/$25/$40 Drug Card	**HMO** $2,500/$5,000 Deductible $30/$50 Office Visit Co-pay $500 Inpatient Co-pay $250 Outpatient Co-pay 100% $5,000/$10,000 MOOP $15/$35/$60 Drug Card
MONTHLY COSTS Employee Only $440 Employee and Family $1,300	**MONTHLY COSTS** Employee Only $260 Employee and Family $770	**MONTHLY COSTS** Employee Only $140 Employee and Family $410
EE CONTRIBUTION Employee Only $180 Employee and Family $530	**EE CONTRIBUTION** Employee Only $90 Employee and Family $170	**EE CONTRIBUTION** Employee Only $0 Employee and Family $0
	ER HRA CONTRIBUTION Employee Only $1,000 Employee and Family $2,000	**ER HSA CONTRIBUTION** Employee Only $1,000 Employee and Family $2,000

This is a *Triple Option* scenario. This scenario paints a picture of all three options being available now and for the foreseeable future. Employees who chose the old fashioned managed care plan will pay the highest employee contribution thus allowing the employer to control their overall cost. Employees who have elected the cost-sharing plan will share in an employer funded HRA account to help compensate for the additional but hypothetical liability the program creates. They will pay a lesser contribution than the employees who select the managed care option but they will be entitled to an HRA account containing employer dollars equal to two-thirds of the deductible. Again, the additional liability only comes into play if the employee receives inpatient or outpatient hospital care (generally speaking, care outside the realm of an office visit). Employees who have elected the consumer directed healthcare or deductible-first program will receive a fully vested employer contribution that is the employee's money from day one.

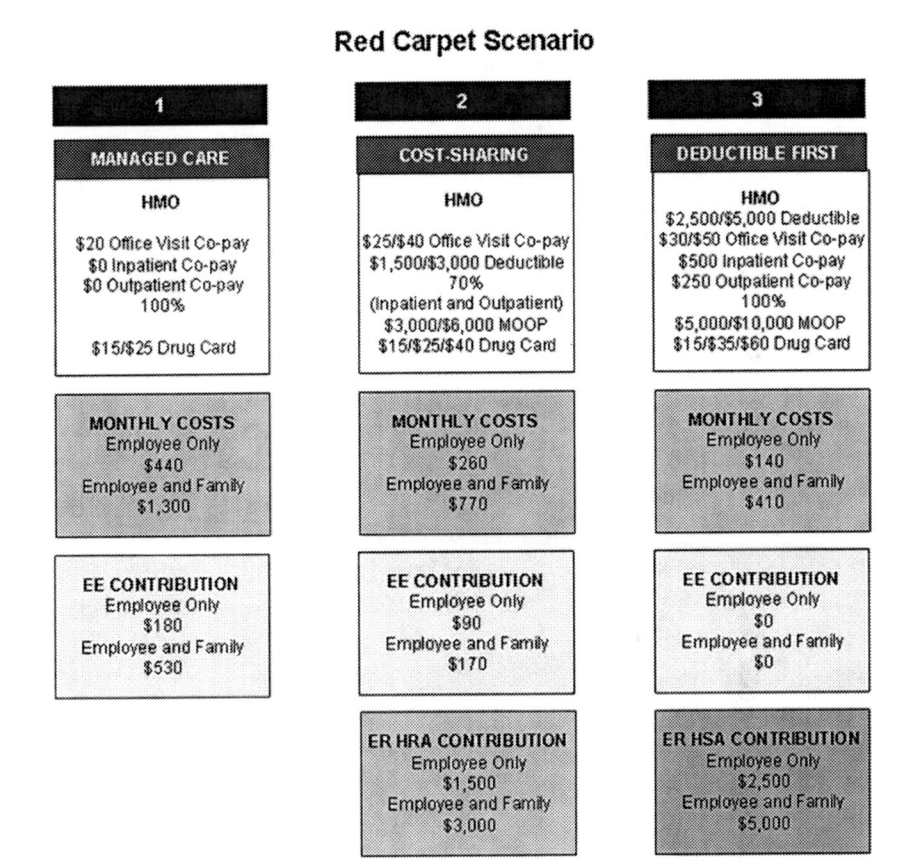

Red Carpet Scenario

1	2	3
MANAGED CARE	**COST-SHARING**	**DEDUCTIBLE FIRST**
HMO $20 Office Visit Co-pay $0 Inpatient Co-pay $0 Outpatient Co-pay 100% $15/$25 Drug Card	HMO $25/$40 Office Visit Co-pay $1,500/$3,000 Deductible 70% (Inpatient and Outpatient) $3,000/$6,000 MOOP $15/$25/$40 Drug Card	HMO $2,500/$5,000 Deductible $30/$50 Office Visit Co-pay $500 Inpatient Co-pay $250 Outpatient Co-pay 100% $5,000/$10,000 MOOP $15/$35/$60 Drug Card
MONTHLY COSTS Employee Only $440 Employee and Family $1,300	**MONTHLY COSTS** Employee Only $260 Employee and Family $770	**MONTHLY COSTS** Employee Only $140 Employee and Family $410
EE CONTRIBUTION Employee Only $180 Employee and Family $530	**EE CONTRIBUTION** Employee Only $90 Employee and Family $170	**EE CONTRIBUTION** Employee Only $0 Employee and Family $0
	ER HRA CONTRIBUTION Employee Only $1,500 Employee and Family $3,000	**ER HSA CONTRIBUTION** Employee Only $2,500 Employee and Family $5,000

Let's assume for a second this employer previously maintained only the managed care offering, which studies show close to 80% of employers do. All three options here create what the majority will perceive to be a win-win for both the employer and the employee. In any of the two "new" options, the employer and the employee will pay less but employees will also share in the employer's savings by way of an HRA or HSA contribution.

Now let's move on to the *Red Carpet* scenario. In this scenario, the big payoff for employees is in the deductible-first option. Employees are moved down the "carpet" which has been, for all intents and purposes, rolled out leading to the deductible-first option, consumer directed healthcare. This scenario exemplifies the much-needed mantra. *Make it cheap. Make it easy.* Again with this example, employees who chose the old fashioned managed care plan will pay the highest employee contribution thus allowing the employer to control their overall cost. Employees who have elected the cost-sharing plan will share in an employer funded HRA account to help compensate for the additional liability of the program but this time, the deductible is fully funded. This is done to create a sense of comfort in enrolling in a plan with the knowledge that, for now, the employer is picking up the difference, so to speak. They will pay a lesser contribution than the employees who select the managed care option.

The consumer directed healthcare option is clearly the best option and is ridiculously attractive in order to bolster enrollment. The deductible is fully funded by way of an employer contribution to the employee owned HSA. The employer still pays less than the managed care premium overall but the employer obtains the enrollment required. Under this scenario, the employer banks on the future and retains his rights to the long overdue healthcare savings to future years. Employees participating in the consumer directed option should only receive the full employer funding for the first year of the plan. It should be scaled back or eliminated in future years. This scenario works best to achieve a continued progression towards consumer directed healthcare without having employees left feeling shuttled around like cattle.

Another concept that can be beta-tested as consumer directed healthcare moves to the forefront is the notion of allowing employees to defer compensation to a following year. In other words, employees could agree to have a small percentage of earnings deferred to the following year and then taken from their payroll pre-tax to fund the HSA in Year Two.

Disney Method

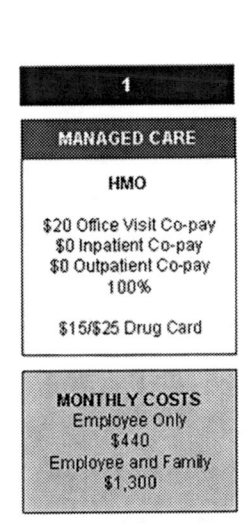

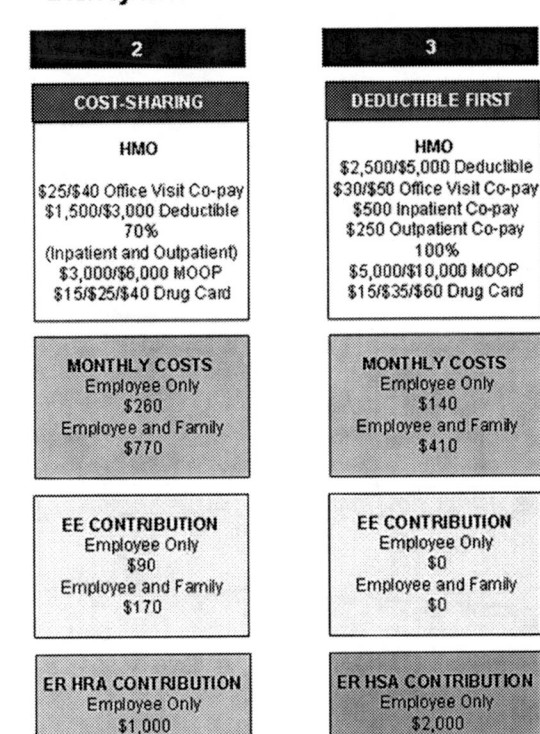

1. MANAGED CARE

HMO
$20 Office Visit Co-pay
$0 Inpatient Co-pay
$0 Outpatient Co-pay
100%

$15/$25 Drug Card

MONTHLY COSTS
Employee Only
$440
Employee and Family
$1,300

EE CONTRIBUTION
Employee Only
$180
Employee and Family
$530

2. COST-SHARING

HMO
$25/$40 Office Visit Co-pay
$1,500/$3,000 Deductible
70%
(Inpatient and Outpatient)
$3,000/$6,000 MOOP
$15/$25/$40 Drug Card

MONTHLY COSTS
Employee Only
$260
Employee and Family
$770

EE CONTRIBUTION
Employee Only
$90
Employee and Family
$170

ER HRA CONTRIBUTION
Employee Only
$1,000
Employee and Family
$2,000

3. DEDUCTIBLE FIRST

HMO
$2,500/$5,000 Deductible
$30/$50 Office Visit Co-pay
$500 Inpatient Co-pay
$250 Outpatient Co-pay
100%
$5,000/$10,000 MOOP
$15/$35/$60 Drug Card

MONTHLY COSTS
Employee Only
$140
Employee and Family
$410

EE CONTRIBUTION
Employee Only
$0
Employee and Family
$0

ER HSA CONTRIBUTION
Employee Only
$2,000
Employee and Family
$4,000

Next up is the *Disney Method*. In this scenario, employees are moved along towards consumer directed healthcare but incrementally. Much like the lines at Disney, there are sights and "achievement points" along the way. Ever been to Disney? Guests just don't wait in endless lines until they board the ride or attraction. There are exhibits, films and things to see along the way. This scenario works in the same fashion. It is designed to achieve comfort in the minds of the employees incrementally. Employees start off in managed care, then move to the cost-sharing/HRA combination and then finally to the deductible/first/employer funded HSA program. Again with this example, employees who chose the old fashioned managed care plan will pay the highest employee contribution and the contribution becomes less and less expensive as employees move towards consumer directed healthcare.

The consumer directed healthcare option is clearly the best option and the employer nicely funds the HSA in the first year. This example will work best for a workforce that will respond to change but on their own terms and their own pace. All options can be offered in conjunction with one another or the employer can chose to only offer the managed care in year one, only the cost-sharing in year two and only the consumer direction program in the third and final year. If that route of implementation is chosen, employees will be given an overview of the three-year strategy so they come to expect the following years' changes and are educated during the entire strategic timeframe as to the benefits and know-how of consumer directed healthcare.

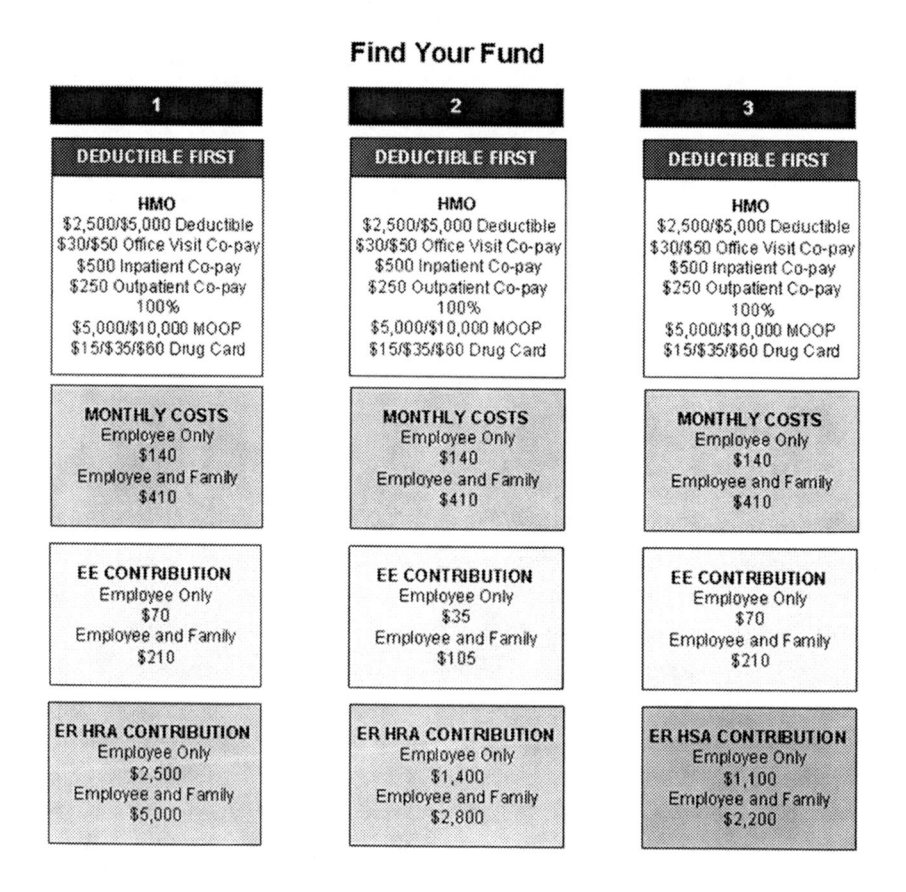

Find Your Fund

1	2	3
DEDUCTIBLE FIRST	**DEDUCTIBLE FIRST**	**DEDUCTIBLE FIRST**
HMO $2,500/$5,000 Deductible $30/$50 Office Visit Co-pay $500 Inpatient Co-pay $250 Outpatient Co-pay 100% $5,000/$10,000 MOOP $15/$35/$60 Drug Card	**HMO** $2,500/$5,000 Deductible $30/$50 Office Visit Co-pay $500 Inpatient Co-pay $250 Outpatient Co-pay 100% $5,000/$10,000 MOOP $15/$35/$60 Drug Card	**HMO** $2,500/$5,000 Deductible $30/$50 Office Visit Co-pay $500 Inpatient Co-pay $250 Outpatient Co-pay 100% $5,000/$10,000 MOOP $15/$35/$60 Drug Card
MONTHLY COSTS Employee Only $140 Employee and Family $410	**MONTHLY COSTS** Employee Only $140 Employee and Family $410	**MONTHLY COSTS** Employee Only $140 Employee and Family $410
EE CONTRIBUTION Employee Only $70 Employee and Family $210	**EE CONTRIBUTION** Employee Only $35 Employee and Family $105	**EE CONTRIBUTION** Employee Only $70 Employee and Family $210
ER HRA CONTRIBUTION Employee Only $2,500 Employee and Family $5,000	**ER HRA CONTRIBUTION** Employee Only $1,400 Employee and Family $2,800	**ER HSA CONTRIBUTION** Employee Only $1,100 Employee and Family $2,200

Next up is the *Find Your Fund* scenario. In this scenario, deductible-first health insurance is implemented immediately. Employees do not make choices based upon plan design but are provided a choice of a different kind. What type of employer funding on how much employer funding do I want? Keep in mind, the minimum deductible in a HSA-eligible deductible-first plan is $1,100 in 2007. Employees can choose to have the entire deductible funded by the employer via an HRA. This choice would only allow them to contribute $350 to an HSA as the HRA contribution would deduct from the maximum pre-tax contribution allowable under an HSA. The second choice would be for an employee to open an HSA account, fund the minimum deductible of $1,100 with his or her own pre-tax dollars and then participate in an HRA that would use the employer's money. The employer's money would prospectively fund the difference between the minimum deductible of $1,100 and the program's actual deductible of $2,500.

The last option lends itself more to the true spirit of consumer directed healthcare. In this option, employees would receive an employer contribution to their HSA in an amount equal to the 2007 minimum deductible of $1,100. Employees would have ownership of the employer contribution for immediate or future use but would also be responsible for funding the difference between the employer's contribution of $1,100 and the program's actual deductible of $2,500.

If an employer has a workforce that lends itself to fairly painless comprehension of new concepts such as the one outlined above, this would be the best option we've discussed so far. It implements many of the attributes of this concept right away while maintaining some semblance of a "get-to-know you" process while the employer's money is still in the game on a variety of different levels. Employees can immediately begin to experience consumer directed healthcare but from a comfortable distance should they chose.

One or The Other

1

DEDUCTIBLE FIRST

HMO
$2,500/$5,000 Deductible
$30/$50 Office Visit Co-pay
$500 Inpatient Co-pay
$250 Outpatient Co-pay
100%
$5,000/$10,000 MOOP
$15/$35/$60 Drug Card

MONTHLY COSTS
Employee Only
$140
Employee and Family
$410

EE CONTRIBUTION
Employee Only
$35
Employee and Family
$105

ER HRA CONTRIBUTION
Employee Only
$1,400
Employee and Family
$2,800

2

DEDUCTIBLE FIRST

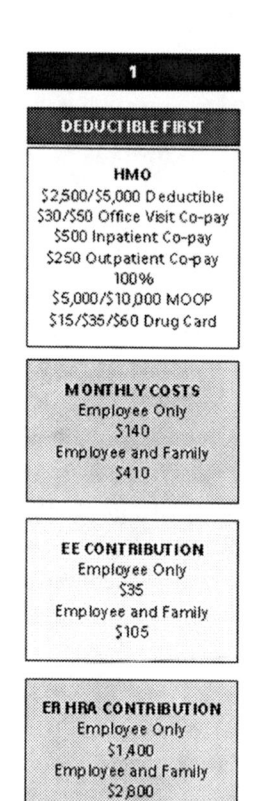

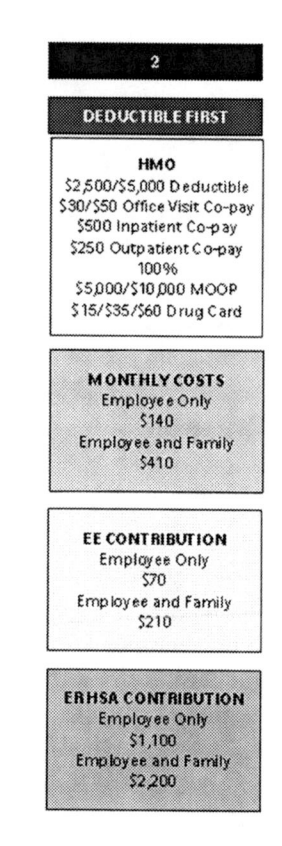

HMO
$2,500/$5,000 Deductible
$30/$50 Office Visit Co-pay
$500 Inpatient Co-pay
$250 Outpatient Co-pay
100%
$5,000/$10,000 MOOP
$15/$35/$60 Drug Card

MONTHLY COSTS
Employee Only
$140
Employee and Family
$410

EE CONTRIBUTION
Employee Only
$70
Employee and Family
$210

ER HSA CONTRIBUTION
Employee Only
$1,100
Employee and Family
$2,200

Lastly, there is the *One Or The Other* scenario. In this scenario, deductible-first health insurance is implemented immediately as well and employees are left with the latter two choice of the *Find Your Fund* scenario. It becomes a question of do the employees want their liability on the front-end or the back-end of the deductible-first? The first choice would this time assume an employee opens an HSA account, funds the 2007 minimum deductible of $1,100 with his or her own pre-tax dollars and then participates in an HRA that would use the employer's money. The employer's money would again prospectively fund the difference between the minimum deductible of $1,100 and the program's actual deductible of $2,500. The employee selecting this option would prefer front-end liability.

The other option would assume the employee selecting it would prefer back-end liability. In this option, employees would receive an employer contribution to their HSA in an amount equal to the 2007 minimum deductible of $1,100. Employees would again have ownership of the employer contribution for immediate or future use but would also be responsible for funding the difference between the employer's contribution of $1,100 and the program's actual deductible of $2,500. In other words, this employee would assume the liability on the back-end.

5.9 What You Won't See

As can be easily derived from the previous sections, there is no right way to do this other than the way employers feel will work best based upon their understanding, tolerance and comprehension levels of their respective workforce. We toyed with the idea of including a section in this text to address that exact point. We were going to call it: Meet The New Guy, The Full Monte or Slow and Steady. Within the section we were going to debate and discuss whether it is best to implement consumer directed healthcare first as an option, implement it as the only option right away or implement it incrementally over a pre-determined amount of time. The conclusion we came to is probably the right and only conclusion: it depends. The best way to implement consumer directed healthcare is up to each employer and the type of workforce they have.

With any change regardless of how it is implemented, it will be met with unfounded criticism and speculative concern. With that in mind, we wanted to remind you of the extensive research we performed in preparing this text. It is also important to note, the genesis of our research was true and pure in nature. We did not set out to prove or substantiate a pre-determined opinion. Consumer directed healthcare was on the horizon and we set out to find out as much as we could about it, good and bad. What we found was good and the tone of nearly every article, survey, analysis or report on this subject is positive, upbeat and enthusiastic about the prospect of change.

Having said that, we wanted to leave behind some ammunition for use against those who contradict the majority opinion that this is a concept to embrace. Humana, a national medical insurer, produced a report on its own members that are enrolled currently in a consumer directed healthcare program. The report validated that:

- Premium increases remained in the single digits as compared to the national average double-digits (managed care).

- Claim trend was lowered to 5%-6% as compared to the national average of 12%-14%.
- A savings of $625 per employee was generated.
- Premium savings was achieved without limiting options and healthcare plan choices.
- Prescription drug use for chronic illness was in line with national averages. In other words, consumers are not abandoning their treatment plans due to the up-front liability of a deductible.
- Employer-sponsored benefits had become predictable as the result of more stable and controlled premium increases.
- The use of preventive care was on par with national averages.

5.10 If It Ain't Broke, Steal It

There must be several, constant criteria in place for a consumer directed healthcare plan to be rolled out effectively. As there is not an abundance of real-world experience, here is what others who have already embraced and implemented this concept have learned so far. After all, there is nothing more valuable than an education provided by other companies' mistakes.

This is not an overnight success story. We have experienced enrollment to be scarce at first leading employers to rely upon the attractiveness of employer funding and positive word-of-mouth from the early adopters. Consumer directed healthcare can reach its "tipping point" at any organization provided employers adopt the following manta. *Make it cheap. Make it easy.* That and fund, fund, fund 'till Daddy takes the T-bird away.

Make it easy to understand. We've been taught to fear what we don't understand, especially when we think we might be "losing" something. As we've discussed, sellers don't sell what they don't understand and buyers don't buy what they don't understand. Provide the necessary tools and explain this concept and its products over and over again for as long as it takes to each and every employee until they are positioned to embrace it. Your employees and your bottom line will eventually thank you.

There is only thing more valuable than effective communication and that's effective over-communication. They say people need to exhibit a new behavior fifty times before it becomes second nature. So don't expect to have a fully engaged workforce after an employee meeting one afternoon. This will consume more up-front time for Human Resources but the payoff is employees will truly understand their health insurance program. The up-front time will payoff in reduced time spent squashing problems or resolving conflicts with employees who misunderstood their coverage on the back-end. Communicate early, regularly and often.

Employers and their chosen insurers must have the tools to allow employees to fully embrace this healthcare concept. Employees must know how to effectively and accurately budget for annual healthcare expenses so they feel prepared. During the year, they need knowledge of how to shop for price and quality so they can come to demand value for their healthcare dollar. They need to know how to achieve a healthy lifestyle and receive the motivation required to sustain one as well.

Reward the proper behaviors, the behaviors conducive to consumer directed healthcare and not to mention a healthy, productive workforce. It is a known fact that if you want to fix the big problems for good, you have to first eliminate the small problems. For example, mayors who want to reduce crime in their city first replace the broken windows and eliminate graffiti on their buildings. In other words, they establish an environment that is no longer conducive or inviting to larger crimes. The same is true for healthcare concepts. For employees to grasp the big picture, they must first see the smaller picture in their own lives and their own attitude and behaviors towards healthcare and health insurance.

5.11 If We Were In Charge

This healthcare concept can seem like a jagged little pill consumers know they need to swallow to improve the health of our current system. Hopefully, this text outlined the groundwork required to obtain employee engagement of the big picture. Even still, if we were in charge, we would legislate a running head start. We would allow consumers to establish an HSA even if they are not covered by deductible-first or high deductible health insurance. In other words, consumers could make deposits but not withdraw from their HSA until they obtained the necessary deductible-first program. This would allow employers to notify and educate their workforce as to a future health insurance change. Employees would then have ample time to get on board and prepare for the upcoming shift in coverage.

Peer pressure is an incredible motivator, just ask any teenager. In other words, Government should require employers to have a consumer directed healthcare program much like they required an HMO offering at the onset of managed care. This would serve to diminish the wait-and-see approach many cautious employers will feel forced to adopt. If all employers were required to maintain a suitable option this would level the playing field and allow employers the opportunity to institute this movement at their companies without fear of current or prospective employee attrition.

About the Authors

Jeffrey Ingalls is the President of The Stratford Financial Group. Jeffrey has spent his sixteen-year insurance career solely within the realm of employee benefits. Jeffrey is the host of a weekly radio broadcast, "For Your Benefit" on which he discusses topics relative to employee benefits live each Sunday morning. Jeffrey lives in Cedar Grove, New Jersey with his wife, Lisa and his three children; Atticus, Holden and Denham.

Daniel Ritter is the Chief Executive Officer and owner of The Stratford Financial Group. Daniel's insurance experience spans the gamut from individual life insurance to employee benefits and everything in-between. His peers consider Daniel the consummate entrepreneur and while his insurance career spans over twenty-one years, he founded The Stratford Financial Group in 1997. Daniel resides in Basking Ridge, New Jersey with his wife, Lisa and two children; Kevin and Alyssa.

"For Your Benefit"
Listen LIVE at:
www.wmtram.com
CLASSIC
wmtram.com
WMTR
1250 AM
OLDIES
Sundays 9AM EST

978-0-595-42985-1
0-595-42985-8